So
You
Want
to Be
a
PSYCHIC
INTUITIVE?

© Kyle Cassidy

About the Author

Alexandra Chauran is a second generation professional fortune teller. She has been reading the crystal ball professionally since 1999. Holding a Master's Degree in Teaching from Seattle University, she enjoys building carefully upon what is already understood by the student and she offers an apprentice internship to her local practice in the greater Seattle area. Alexandra is also proficient in other forms of divination.

To Write to the Author

If you wish to contact the author or would like more information about this book, please write to the author in care of Llewellyn Worldwide, and we will forward your request. Both the author and publisher appreciate hearing from you and learning of your enjoyment of this book and how it has helped you. Llewellyn Worldwide cannot guarantee that every letter written to the author can be answered, but all will be forwarded. Please write to:

Alexandra Chauran
℅ Llewellyn Worldwide
2143 Wooddale Drive
Woodbury, MN 55125-2989

Please enclose a self-addressed stamped envelope for reply,
or $1.00 to cover costs. If outside the USA, enclose
an international postal reply coupon.

So You Want to Be a PSYCHIC INTUITIVE?

A Down-to-Earth Guide

Alexandra Chauran

Llewellyn Publications
Woodbury, Minnesota

FIRST EDITION
First Printing, 2012

Book design by Bob Gaul
Cover art: Background image © iStockphoto.com/Jamie Carroll
Cover design by Kevin R. Brown
Editing by Laura Graves

Llewellyn is a registered trademark of Llewellyn Worldwide Ltd.

Library of Congress Cataloging-in-Publication Data
Chauran, Alexandra, 1981–
  So you want to be a psychic intuitive?: a down-to-earth guide/Alexandra Chauran.—1st ed.
    p. cm.
  Includes bibliographical references (p.   ).
  ISBN 978-0-7387-3065-3
1. Psychics. 2. Parapsychology. 3. Intuition. I. Title.
  BF1040.C44 2012
  133.8—dc23
                          2011050488

Llewellyn Publications
A Division of Llewellyn Worldwide Ltd.
2143 Wooddale Drive
Woodbury, MN 55125-2989
www.llewellyn.com

Printed in the United States of America

Contents

Dedication

So You Want to Be a Psychic Intuitive? is dedicated to my mother, who first encouraged me to trust my intuition; to my husband, who used psychic pendulum dowsing to psychically determine our baby's gender while I was pregnant and who put up with me writing this book while she was a newborn; and to my daughter, about whose future I am constantly dreaming.

Introduction

Common Experiences

Sorting through some old clothes in the closet, you stumble across a t-shirt that you wore every week in high school. As you hold it up to view the front, the old cloth soft on your fingertips, your mind is instantly flooded with flashes of memories. Friends laughing, enemies jeering, an old buddy stealing a slice of pizza off your plate. For a brief moment, you allow yourself to wonder what has happened to that buddy, even though you know that you could get back in touch if either of you wanted. Suddenly, your telephone rings and a familiar voice greets your ears. "I was just thinking of you..." And it's your buddy.

We've all had those seemingly psychic moments, haven't we? Have you worried about a family member just in time to catch him or her during a tough time? Have you avoided getting on the freeway just before a major accident blocked all the roads for miles? Have you experienced love at first sight? Most importantly, does one person have more of these coincidences happen than another, and do having experiences like these make you special?

What is a psychic, and why would you want to be one?

The definition of "psychic" in everyday speech in popular culture seems to change fluidly. When an annoyed friend shouts "I'm not psychic," he or she most likely means that mind reading is not a reasonable assumption, and that you have not clearly communicated verbal instructions. But being a psychic is a bit more (and in a way a bit less) than the mentalist party trick of being able to correctly guess what a person is thinking. In this book, we will explore the concept of a psychic as being a person who is in tune with phenomena or information that is perceived from non-physical or even supernatural sources.

Popular science states that we only use ten percent of our brains, and while that is not technically true, you can think of psychic work as a way to access the other ninety percent. The other ninety has not only a great stored memory but stored knowledge and perhaps instinct that can be thought of as the collective wisdom of millions of years of evolution, or perhaps even a product of our society and culture.

Why would anyone, particularly you, want to be a psychic? Chances are that you didn't arrive at the desire to be a psychic out of the blue. I would guess that the most common reason for wanting to be a psychic is that you're a little bit psychic already, and you'd love to be able to develop those abilities into real skills and talents, rather than just another reason to be teased by your family and friends or to be paranoid about this strange and often dangerous world in which we live today.

Thinking that you might already be a little psychic is a perfectly acceptable reason to want to be a psychic. Getting to know yourself is certainly a more lofty goal than to want to be a psychic because you saw one on television and thought this was a good way to become rich and famous. In our culture, we are often encouraged to laugh away those things that are strange, or at best, encouraged to capitalize on being so strange that we are considered freakish.

In my opinion, another good reason to want to become a psychic is the desire to help other people. But why would one dedicate their life to helping people in this way if everyone has psychic moments? Because being a psychic, walking the line between the real and the unreal, can be an exciting experience, and can help you become a hero among friends and strangers. The idea of journeying to a place unseen by most people and bringing back kernels of knowledge, truth, and wisdom is one that has been played out by archetypical heroes in stories throughout time. The archetypical hero's journey is the work of the Shaman.

In many cultures, a Shaman is one who can enter a trance or a world others cannot share, speak with the dead, or discover messages from the divine. Sometimes a Shaman will even take a sickness or an affliction upon himself or herself in order to spare another person. All of this work might be frightening to some people. If you have the nerve or the belief system that allows you to feel at peace with your reality melting away before your eyes, and you wish to allow that to happen in order to help others who cannot or will not do it themselves, this is certainly a noble reason to want to be a psychic.

I think that all of the above reasons explain why I wanted to become a psychic myself (yes, even the one that involved fame and fortune.) Since there aren't any sports cars in my driveway nor celebrities beating down my door, I think it is now evident which of my initial reasons were more enduring and fulfilling than foolish daydreams.

I had a healthy dose of prior experience with psychic flashes. A psychic flash is an instant in time during which you feel flooded with information that might be perceived through your senses or just understood in your mind. Since my mother is now a professional psychic herself (amongst other amazing accomplishments), such things were so encouraged in me as a child that they were treated as routine and mundane occurrences in our household. Rather than being made to feel discouraged or dismissed, as might have happened with another mother, I felt confident and curious about those times when I anticipated a future event, shared a dream that had meaning, or experimented with tools of divination as a child.

Before I became a professional, or even began to attempt to help others, I started to use psychic work as part of my own personal spiritual path. Even if you prefer to use your skills and talents to help others, I encourage you to begin by learning how to help yourself. The biggest reason for this is because you should be able to help yourself to become a better person before you start trying to fix the lives of others. As the urgent instruction for airline safety goes, "please affix your own oxygen mask before attempting to help others." If you are trying to serve those around you because you have a sore spot or an empty hole in your own life, you will not be successful.

Another practical reason to start with yourself is to allow you to make little mistakes, or learn the nuances of your own personal practice before stumbling through a psychic reading with another person. If you jump straight into the potential of being criticized by others before you have gotten the hang of things, you might be more easily discouraged by the little failures that happen along the way than if you do a bit of practice on your own life first to gain confidence and momentum. Besides, you're always there and hopefully willing to share deep personal problems with yourself that you honestly want to resolve. You can easily meet hundreds of other people who say they want help with an issue who really don't want to solve the problem at all. Confusion about motives can set up some pretty big mental blocks that might in turn confuse you about your own abilities. As a beginner, it is hard to know where your own limitations begin when someone is sub-consciously sabotaging your efforts.

I worked hard on my own problems at first, and then branched out to help family, close friends, and spiritual peers. Later, I found that I wanted to reach out to even more people, and so I did, starting my own small business as a psychic. When I grew up and went to college, I pursued my psychic goals in the same way I did my academic ones: reading books, approaching experts, joining professional organizations, and of course, by practicing daily.

I gave myself little homework assignments to push myself to grow outside of my comfort zone. And this practice continues to be instrumental in my growth as a psychic, and indeed in my progress in other areas of my life. For that reason, I will suggest homework for you as well with each chapter, but I encourage you to give yourself extra-credit work of your own. Create goals for yourself. The best goals can be formed using the acronym **SMART** which stands for: Specific, Measurable, Attainable, Realistic, and Timely.

What you will learn from this book

So You Want To Be A Psychic Intuitive? will help you understand more about the potential psychic abilities that you already have, and to embrace what it means to be a psychic for you. By following the tips and homework applications, you will be able to begin immediately tapping into your own intuition, look for signs from mysterious sources that may already be all around you, listen to messages that may be conveyed to you, and pass along those messages to others who are not yet developing their own psychic talents. Best of all, you'll begin to use your own psychic connections as a resource to answer specific questions in your life and in the lives of others.

....

Homework
Solo

Find a journal to use throughout this book and beyond as you grow as a psychic. Start out by writing down the reasons you would like to become a psychic. Your reasons might change as you learn more about what you can and cannot actually do, so be honest and thorough as you write out your hopes and dreams. The worst-case scenario is that you'll have a little chuckle at yourself when you inevitably revise it later to include new goals that may be quite different... and much more realistic.

If you have had psychic experiences in the past, write down your recollection of those events. Hopefully, noticing your strengths and patterns will help you know where to begin stretching your existing talents and give you some confidence that will boost your motivation to work hard on developing new skills.

With a Partner

Working with a partner may be a bit of a challenge for those who haven't yet built an understanding support system of people who love you for all of your quirks and abilities. If you do, try talking to them about your ambitions and asking for input about strengths they see in you. Perhaps a parent can tell you about intuitive moments you've had since childhood. A significant other might be able to point out that you have a good heart for helping people in need. Often we need others to be mirrors to ourselves to help our self-esteem grow, so use this homework assignment as an excuse to list those strengths of yours that shine through to those around you.

1 Get Ready, Get Set, Go!

The Different Types of Psychics

Not all psychics are created equal. Each of us sees the world differently through the filters of our own perceptions, culture, and experience. The way we understand the otherworldly is similarly varied. So, even if two psychics were performing a psychic reading on the same person and the same topic, they might see the same answer in two completely different ways.

The terminology for these different ways of sensing things is often organized under the prefix "clair-" meaning "clear," followed by a suffix that indicates a sense. For example, "clairvoyant" means "clear seeing" while "clairaudient" means "clear hearing." They are names for the kinds of psychics that see visions or hear messages respectively.

The "clair-" prefix can be added onto touch, taste, or smell as clairtangency, clairgustance, and clairsalience, but such terms are more rarely in use. Nobody is going to quiz you on the semantics of being a psychic.

Categorizing yourself becomes less important as you grow more familiar with the way you work, but it is important to recognize your strengths as a beginner. If you are a visual-type person, you could bang your head against the wall all day long trying to hear voices from the beyond, or you could jump right in and learn to see visions right away. Chapter one will give you a sense of what kind of psychic ability you might have, and help you through the process of how to recognize messages. Each exercise will help you tune into your senses.

Your Six Senses

You've heard the colloquial term "the sixth sense," which refers to the gut feeling one experiences, and not an actual perception. Your sixth sense is more of an understanding, or an emotional reaction to no perceptions at all. Imagine that you were about to walk home from an acquaintance's house at night, along a route that you had traveled many times before, but this time you suddenly felt very uneasy. You found yourself making excuses to stay a little longer, dragging out conversation by the doorway with your coat on, even as your host politely waits for you to leave. Would you listen to this "bad feeling" you were having and arrange to get a ride home? In this case, your sixth sense is actually a fearful or emotional state of mind.

Imagine now that you were attempting to decide in which school you should enroll your child who has special needs. After visiting several schools, each one seemingly as good as the other, you still wonder about how to make the best choice for your child. After stopping for a brief moment to pray, asking for guidance from the divine to help you make the right choice, the name of one of the schools pops suddenly into your head. The decision seems perfectly clear to you, as if it would be strange that you ever had trouble deciding in the first place. In this example, the sixth sense is actually just intuition—knowing the right answer and trusting it completely.

The sixth sense can also refer to the way that intuition interacts with your mind to form perceptions. Examples include seeing visions or visualizing with your mind's eye. Each of your existing five senses can interact with your psychic mind to help you understand messages whether you are literally or figuratively using them at all. Let's go over your five senses to see how they might work with your psychic talents. If one or more of them doesn't seem to work for you, you might easily compensate with another and still be a great psychic.

Clairvoyance

James had seen faces in everything since he was a little kid. He'd see faces in the leaves in the trees, or in the swirls of wood grain on a door. Sometimes he would even point out to a friend how a car looked like it had a funny face, showing where the eyes and the mouth would be, causing the friend to laugh and agree, seeing now what James had seen all along. So, it was no surprise to James that when he started trying to talk to ghosts, he could see them. In fact, James worked hard in order to find ways to see them by looking in a crystal that had as many swirls as wood grain, or water that had as many movements as the waving leaves on trees.

Seeing things didn't scare James. For him, it wasn't as if people were literally leaping out of his divination tools. In reality they were simply images his mind drew from random things. He was aware of this fact, and it didn't make his psychic work any less effective. Sure, James was letting his brain connect the dots, but he believed that the dead people he contacted were what influenced the random arrangement that inspired his eyes. He felt privileged to be able to work with them in these ways, but he knew that his divination tools were just a crutch. He didn't need them. In fact, if he found himself wishing to talk with a ghost without his usual divination supplies, he knew that he could just close his eyes and see them in his mind's eye.

His friends would sometimes ask James to contact their dead relatives. James would simply look in his crystal ball or bowl of water, and start describing the people he saw. He'd wait until he picked out eyes and a mouth in his divination medium of choice, and then look where the nose and hair would be. If the hair was dark, he'd say it was brown or black. By then, his friends would recognize which relative it was. If it was light, he'd say it was blonde or gray. He'd mention if the lips or nose were big or thin. As he became more skilled with this, he would be able to pick up other images. Sometimes the faces would hold up something in their hands, and James would be able to communicate that message to his friends. One dead relative might hold up a musical note to encourage his friend's musical pursuits. Another might hold a cross to warn his other friend against his tendency to skip going to church on Sundays. James was a clairvoyant.

Clairvoyance is the ability to see psychic pictures. Clairvoyant visions might be seen in dreams, or seen in your imagination or mind's eye. The visions might come in a flash, as if seen with your real eyes like you are watching a scene in a movie. Seeing auras—halos of colored light around people—can be a form of clairvoyance. Or, visions might simply be symbols that are seen in a scrying divination tool. Scrying is when a psychic looks for pictures in an object such as a crystal ball, a bowl of milk or water, or a candle flame. In my personal experience working with American psychic colleagues, clairvoyance seems to be the most common psychic sense. The popularity of clairvoyance might be because we are encouraged to be visual learners in our school system, constantly shown visual aids and using reading to learn from textbooks. This visual emphasis continues in our adult lives as we stare at television and computer screens.

Clairvoyant Exercises

Chances are that you too are a visual learner, to some extent, if you exist in American culture; able to call to mind the idea of a color, shape, or face of a loved one with ease. If you have advanced visualization skills like being able to imagine what your home looks like from above, even if you haven't ever flown over it, so much the better. People who dream in color also have the added bonus of interpreting the colors symbolically.

If you are already quite skilled at calling a picture to your mind, then a good way to develop your clairvoyance is to branch out into scrying with a dark bowl full of water, a bowl of milk, a lit candle, a crystal ball, or a scrying mirror. Scrying is the art of using a tool in order to search for images that your eyes or mind's eye can see psychically. Scrying is an important exercise for the budding clairvoyant because it gives an appropriate time and place to see visions in abundance without them becoming elusive or disruptive.

If you are not a visual learner, you will have a hard time holding the picture of even the face of somebody you see every day in your mind. You probably can't picture a set of directions like turning left or right at landmarks as maps or actual courses of travel in your mind. You're not alone. I have a hard time with each of the tasks listed above but I am still excellent at scrying, having even written a book about crystal ball reading. Seeing visions can be a learned skill, and you can start advancing your own clairvoyance by meditating using visualization as described further in the following chapter's section on meditation.

Another way to work on your clairvoyance is to attempt to see auras. Auras are often seen by clairvoyants as halos of light that surround a person's entire body and are thought to be a visual representation of energy. By "energy" psychics mean *chi,* the life force that flows through people or even inanimate objects in the universe. Chi is what psychics can sense in various ways including auras. Some clairvoyants can even see the auras of animals, plants, and even non-living things. I suggest that beginners use a willing human being, preferably one who is familiar with manipulating his or her own energy, though anyone willing to sit still and participate will do.

Have your partner wear neutral-colored clothing, such as white, black, or beige and sit against a white wall with plenty of lighting. Ideally you will have natural light available to use for this experiment. The lack of color is important because after staring at a color long enough, the color-sensing areas of your eyes will begin to be so excited from the process that you may see a residual color opposite on the color wheel. So, if you stare at a bright red ball for a while, and then shift your eyes quickly to a white wall, you will see a green ball briefly. You want the auras that you see to be genuinely related to the person who is working with you, rather than just an artifact of your eyesight.

Sit and meditate while staring at your partner. Allow your focus to soften so that you are looking beyond your partner, rather than right at him or her. Ironically, it is harder to see the auras of people that you know very well, possibly because we tend to retract our energy bubbles when we are around people with whom we feel most comfortable. So, for the greatest chance of success, have your partner expand his or her aura by imagining a situation in which he or she would not want people coming close. Perhaps thinking about sitting on a crowded bus, and hoping not to be jostled or touched, or re-imagining a situation in which he or she felt defensive will help.

Allow your eyes to scan the edges of your partner's body from head to toe. You're looking for a slight fuzziness that separates the aura from its surroundings. If your partner is projecting the aura well, it may be extending from the body a few inches to even a few feet. You may even be able to see several colors associated with the aura. The aura may be changing colors rapidly, or there may be different colors hovering around different parts of the body. At this point, I like to sketch auras, so if you have some colored pencils on hand for your experiment, you could produce interesting results for your partner to view. Try sketching again in an hour or a week to note where any changes might be happening. As you do so, you'll begin to see how different colors might shift around affected areas; for example, if your partner has a headache or is recovering from a cold. Colors can vary in meaning from person to person, here are some sample meanings.

Red: Passion, anger, inflammation
Orange: Power, strength, energy
Yellow: Learning, intuition, study
Green: Love, growth, abundance
Blue: Healing, rest, sadness
Purple: Spirituality, wisdom, happiness

If you seem to be unable to see an aura on your partner, you might try another willing partner, as some people subconsciously block the efforts of others to see or influence their energy in any way as an automatic protection mechanism. Or, you may try using your other senses to interact with auras. Some people cannot see auras, but they can feel them with their hands. Read the clairtangent exercises for instructions on how to feel auras.

While we're observing other human beings, the theory behind the meanings of the parts of your body can also help you interpret body language and the poses people take. François Delsarte, an eighteenth-century teacher, discovered a universal system of expression which he wrote about in *Delsarte System of Expression* that gave specific meanings to different parts of the body. Delsarte's system is very useful for you to recognize if you are clairvoyant, and tend to have visions of people or might see them when scrying. However, this can even be used as an extra layer of interpretation for the people depicted on tarot cards, if you choose to explore this divination tool.

Once you grab a willing partner, each of you should familiarize yourselves first with Delsarte's system of expression as described in the meditation in the clairtangent exercise later in this chapter. Delsarte's system can be done as a guided meditation with you reading it aloud to him or her, or you can both do it together after recording it or reading it separately. You should each be familiar with what meaning corresponds to each body part. Now, you can take turns representing meanings by posing your body. You may have to think about how your body appears to your partner, or simply pay attention to how the pose feels to you.

For example, start with each of you taking turns striking an emotional pose. Your pose should not have your arms or legs in front of your torso, since that is an emotional area. Your forearms might be exposed, for example holding arms out and palms up, since each of those body parts also express emotion. Perhaps the legs are bent to draw attention to the lower leg area of emotional expression. If you were to see a person posed like this, sitting or standing or lying down, in a clairvoyant psychic reading, it would show that the person depicted had an emotional link to you or to the person requesting the psychic reading.

Practice again, this time exchanging poses that would depict a message about something in the physical world.

Your hips, shoulders, and jaw may be prominently featured, as each of these body parts represents the physical realm. Seeing a person in a highly physical pose might indicate a protective influence in a person's life or a financial benefactor. Try again to depict a spiritual pose which might indicate a spirit guide for a person or an important religious teacher. Your feet, fingertips, and eyes represent spiritual matters and may be actively engaged in a spiritual pose.

After you've got the idea, you might want to try simply taking turns posing without thinking ahead of time what it might mean. The other partner takes a few minutes to study the pose as if appreciating art, and then suggests what it means. Studying posture is a good way to do a reading of somebody's body language, though not a psychic reading in and of itself. Posing can help both willing parties understand a little more about how we telegraph meaning through our movements. Training yourself to observe a pose leaves you prepared to make quick observations if you see a visionary flash of a human posing in your work as a clairvoyant psychic reader.

Hearing Things

Audrey wasn't afraid of hearing voices. She wasn't scared of being crazy. She knew that it was pretty normal for people to hear things when they wanted to. Audrey had a tendency to talk to herself throughout the day as she went through her ordinary tasks, and she listened carefully to the sounds in nature for signs that were either positive or negative.

Audrey's parents always said that she marched to the beat of a different drummer. And she did. So when she decided that she wanted to start connecting with her spirit guides—non-physical entities she believed provided her with psychic information—she asked them specifically to send her messages she could hear in her everyday life or simply in her mind.

Whenever Audrey's spirit guide wanted to give her a message, she asked to hear an audible sign. Sometimes she would hear a bird chirping in a funny way outside her window, and she'd know that it was time to sit in meditation to contact her spirit guide. Other times, she'd hear a song on the radio with lyrics that seemed to match the thoughts that she was having. One day, she was driving home from work asking herself, "should I quit my job?" The singer on the radio hit a wild guitar riff while he yelled "yeah, yeah, yeah!" Audrey smiled to herself, knowing it was her guide's sense of humor coming through.

When she arrived at home, she grounded herself and then asked her spirit guide to come and get to work giving her answers. In her mind, she heard her spirit guide's voice like a young girl coming from her left-hand side, behind her shoulder, where her guide seemed to usually stand. Audrey kept her eyes closed without turning to the sound of her guide's voice, because that's how she always worked, with sound alone. Her guide's childlike voice was never quite clear. The voice she heard sometimes sounded like there was static in the background, or as if her voice was coming from a great distance or through a tunnel. For that reason, Audrey had to listen very hard, and she sometimes only got pieces of the message anyway.

She asked her spirit guide how she would find another job if she quit her job now. Her spirit guide's voice seemed to be broken up, but came through. "Keep ... right ... keep ... safe. Work hard first." Audrey thought for a moment, and asked if that meant she should keep working this hard job before finding another one. A happy tune went through her head, so she knew that she got it right. Audrey smiled and asked her guide if she would come along on her job hunt and play that same tune again when she was applying for the right job. She heard the cheerful song sound again in agreement, and she thanked her guide, confident that she was on the right track. Audrey is a psychic who hears messages.

While American culture favors visual learners, many cultures support auditory learners, hearing and memorizing through storytelling. As a result, this learning style can be more prevalent in other countries. I am proud to be an auditory learner myself, so if you can repeat many of the lines in your favorite movie, tend to talk to yourself when you do tasks that require concentration, learned how to play an instrument as a child, or can imitate foreign accents well, chances are the hearing part of your brain may also be especially well-tuned to receiving psychic messages.

Clairaudient Exercises

Recall that hearing psychic messages is sometimes called "clairaudience," meaning clear hearing. But, as discussed earlier, it can seem like it is being heard by your physical ears, or may simply just be an imaginary voice in your head in the same way that you "hear" but don't really hear when a song is stuck in your head. Music is also a very frequent way for messages to be conveyed, so even if you don't hear words from your source of psychic information, listen in your mind for a specific tune. The song you hear may be one that is unfamiliar, but conveys an emotion like sadness or happiness. Or, it may be a very familiar song, and the lyrics convey the message accurately. Other sounds may also be perceived, and clairaudience might have been the origin of the knocking sounds that were often reported during mediumship sessions and séances.

In order to develop your psychic ear, that silent receptive meditation can be moved to the early morning as soon as you wake up, or the late evening right before you go to sleep, if you can resist falling asleep at either of those times. As mentioned earlier, the alpha wave state in which your brain is working at these times can make perfectly normal people hear voices. Another way for perfectly normal people to perceive voices or messages is to listen to white noise, like the sound of the shower. Meditating during a rain storm, or by a babbling brook can be helpful, since they provide white noise. Small, affordable tabletop fountains can be useful for meditative purposes.

Touch

Julie was a belly dancer who used the dance form to get in touch with her feminine side as well as to get in tune with her own body. She was also a skilled psychic who believed that her messages came from the divine feminine, a goddess. She only worked with people in person, and she preferred to hold hands with the people for whom she performed psychic readings. She could also sometimes get her psychic messages simply by touching objects.

She spent a lot of time at her local metaphysical bookstore, where the proprietor loved to talk shop about psychic readings. Each time Julie would come into the shop, the store owner would hand her a different rock from the gemstone bin and ask her how she felt about each stone. Julie would clutch each tumbled rock to her heart and squeeze her eyes shut. Sometimes she would feel warmth crawl across her body and a happiness rise in her throat. "Happy rock!" Julie chortled with glee, and the store owner would laugh right along with her in agreement. Another time, she felt a sensation of strength moving up her spine, and she ended up purchasing that stone to make a protection amulet for a friend who needed it in her life.

One day, Julie went to the bookstore to find the shop owner had an unusual request. She had found a ring on the carpet of her shop that looked very valuable. The ring might have slipped right off the finger of a customer, but she did not recognize it, so she didn't know how to return it to its owner. As she dropped the ring into her palm, Julie studied it for a moment before closing her fingers tight around it and holding it to her chest. She squeezed her eyes shut and felt the metal and stone press into her hand, as she recreated the gold and diamond in her mind's eye.

Suddenly, she felt like she was putting on the ring even though she wasn't. The sensation was only in her mind, though it felt so real. She looked down at the hands that were putting on the ring, and realized that they were fat and freckled, instead of her own thin and olive-skinned arms. She realized that she was in someone's bathroom, and she looked up to the mirror in front of her to see a strange face staring back at her. The face was chubby, wore glasses, and the hair was dyed red. Her shirt had a wolf printed on it and she hummed to herself in a high-pitched voice as she felt a comb running through her hair.

Julie shook her head and opened her eyes. Suddenly she was back in the shop with the owner staring expectantly at her as she handed back the ring. As she described the woman with the high-pitched voice that she had seen in her vision, a light of recognition spread across the shop owner's face. That woman was also a regular customer, and she even remembered the wolf t-shirt the woman had been wearing the last time she visited. The shop owner put the ring in an envelope and marked the customer's name on it to be sure to return it the next time that she came in. Though Julie sees visions and hears things, she is also a psychic who relies on the sensation of touch to do her readings.

Imagine touching an object associated with a crime scene—such as the murder weapon—and experiencing a flood of visions in your mind's eye as well as actual sensations of pain that were felt during the horrible act. Sensing psychic messages through touching objects can border on clairvoyance but also rely on your skin making contact with an object that belonged to a specific person or was involved in a significant event. In my experience, I've noticed that psychics who can sense in this way often have a more immersed psychic experience that involves more than one sense, including touch.

Clairtangent Exercises

Start by paying more attention to your body in order to better develop awareness of your sense of touch. Emotions aren't the only things we can feel, and the sensations of pressure, temperature changes, textures, and even itching or pain can be associated with psychic work. Increased heart rate, heavier breathing, or other feelings in your body can also be a part of this. In my experience, it is not the tactile learners or those who learn best by doing who experience this most often. People more likely to sense psychically through touch are those who are body-kinesthetic learners, highly aware of their bodies, such as dancers, martial artists, and other athletes who are good at noticing small changes in their physiology.

Though the list of sensations above may sound unlikely and even scary, it is actually quite common to feel things in conjunction with psychic visions. For example, many people feel sensations in dreams, and some people can feel a temperature drop when the presence of a deceased person or "ghost" enters the room. Even feeling the hairs on the back of your neck stand on end or feeling goosebumps appearing on your arm can be your body's way to tell you to pay attention to your psychic senses. Some psychics use their bodies as a sort of pendulum, sensing the answers to questions through feeling or rocking by first asking what a "yes" and what a "no" might feel like, and then waiting for a physical reaction before proceeding to ask questions. If you tend to find that you feel things easily, this may be a good place to work to improve your psychic ability.

Even for those of us who are not as sensitive with our bodies, we are all susceptible to expressing our subconscious physically. The associations of meanings with specific body parts as written about in *Delsarte System of Expression* not only can be used to understand why there might be a specific feeling in a limb or above your right eye while meditating, but it can also be used to interpret clairvoyant messages that come in the form of a person striking a pose. The following exercise is suitable for a beginner who may not have a lot of body sense.

Start with your normal meditation routine after grounding and centering, and get yourself into silent, receptive meditation. Next, focus on your body while entering meditation by paying attention to your heartbeat and breathing; maintain this focus for a while. Turn your attention to your feet. Your feet represent the spiritual area of your life, in general, but the parts of the feet have correspondences as well. The toes represent the spiritual. The ball of your foot represents the emotional realm, and the heel represent the physical. Make sure that your feet are relaxed, perhaps by first tensing your muscles and then releasing them, before moving on.

The entire vertical column of your body is similarly patterned, so turn your attention to your legs and feet together. Your feet now represent the spiritual, your legs the emotional, and your hips the physical. Notice that there is now some overlap with the meanings of the feet. Now your toe tips are the spiritual-spiritual, the ball of the foot is the spiritual-emotional realm, and the heel is the spiritual-physical world. Relax your legs and hips by tensing the muscles and releasing them if needed.

Now, allow the entire lower part of your body below your hips to represent the physical world since it is rooted to the earth, and draw your attention to your torso. Your torso is now representing the emotional realms, as it contains your heart. Notice that the overlap now between the realms in the lower part of your body has been compounded even further. Allow the muscles in your torso, including your abdomen and back, to relax.

Keep in mind that your torso can be broken down further with even more overlap. The belly where food is digested being physical, the neck and upper chest where air passes through representing the spiritual, and the part in between representing the emotional. A dance teacher once told me of her own psychic feelings whenever her children were hurt. If one of her children is physically injured or bleeding, she feels pain in her belly. If one of her children is suffering from hurt feelings, she feels it above her belly, in the emotional region of her torso.

Allow your attention to focus on your head. Your head as a whole represents the spiritual, but just like your feet, there is going to be some overlap here. Your jaw, since it chews your food, represents the physical. Your cheeks represent the emotional, and your forehead represents the spiritual, since it has your third eye, or your psychic center, at its middle. Your eyes dance along the border of the emotional and the spiritual. Let the muscles in your neck, jaw, and face relax before moving on.

Turn your attention toward your arms. Your shoulders represent the physical, your forearms the emotional, and your hands the spiritual. Relax the muscles in your arms and shoulders. Again, there is overlap with the fingers: the third phalange, the base of the fingers past the knuckle where they connect to your hand is the physical, the segment past the first joint, the second phalange is the emotional and mental, and the very tips, the first phalanges are the spiritual. Make sure the muscles in your hands are relaxed.

Now that you have released your tension and acquainted yourself with your body parts, it is time to use that knowledge in order to sense what realms in your life require the most attention. Sit a while in quiet, receptive meditation and pay attention to your body. You can continue to focus on your breathing or heartbeat, or you can keep taking a roll call of your body parts by letting your attention glide from place to place. As soon as you feel any sensations anywhere, pause and focus on it.

You might sense a warmth or a feeling of coolness in a specific place such as your tummy or a foot. There might be a tickle that would cause you to scratch, or a fuzzy or buzzing feeling. You might even feel almost as if somebody is touching or brushing against you on the shoulder, for example. There are numerous ways that one might sense something through the body. A sensation might always be the same for you, no matter where it happens, or the feelings might be different, and that might be another clue as to the meaning. For example, a cold breeze on your forearm may mean that you are feeling emotionally neglected by a lover, while an electric jolt tapping on your shoulder may be encouragement for you to undertake a fitness routine to take care of your body.

After a few successful practice attempts at "listening" to your body, you can try asking a specific question and feeling for the answer. Hopefully the quality of the feeling in a specific area will clue you in on the answer. Keeping records is especially important because you may notice patterns, such as always feeling a tug at your right elbow when you're wrong and need to listen to an elder's advice.

Another clairtangent exercise that can be done with a partner is to attempt to feel auras, even if you cannot see them. To try this, have your partner sit or lie on the floor and again project his or her aura in order for you to be able to sense it. Close your eyes and begin with your hands several feet away from his or her body, then move them slowly towards his or her head. You may feel a warmth, a fuzzy sensation, or simply have the urge to stop when you find the edge of the aura. Believing that you're actually encountering an aura may be hard if you tend to believe that these things might be just in your head. In that case, test and develop your skills using the following activity I frequently recommend to beginners.

The exercise begins as a simple mirroring game you may have played as a child. Sit facing your partner. Both of you should raise your hands palms out, and bring them close enough to each other that you can feel the heat off of the other person's palms. The distance between your hands may be less than an inch away. Then, one person selected as leader should move his or her palms along the plane between the two of you while the other person mirrors the action. Your movements should be done very slowly. The idea is for the action to become meditative and connecting rather than tricky.

After a time tracing each others' movements, you both should find it becomes easier. When you've each had a turn allowing the act of following the movement to become second nature, you can try moving your hands slightly farther away and continuing the exercise. Bring your hands closer again and both close your eyes. Slow down the movement even more and concentrate on the connection between you two. If another person is available, he or she can act as a quiet observer to see if the two of you are still matching movements with your eyes closed. When you've mastered this, move your hands farther away from each other, perhaps even pushing back your seated position to a short distance away from your partner.

Getting into "the zone" takes some time but once you have, you'll find you can maintain this connection with your eyes closed even when you are several feet away from one another, or even if a wall separates the two of you. Believe it or not, I first learned this "game" at a children's summer camp. I'm pretty convinced it can work for you as long as you have enough patience to find your groove during the slow and boring eyes-open close mirroring portion.

Scents and Tastes

His heritage was very important to him, so Eric had a ceremony he performed daily in order to connect with his ancestors. Each day he brought on offering to his ancestor altar. He poured a libation of rum, water, or palm wine and placed a morsel of food upon it. Today he brought a piece of bread he baked from an old recipe that had been passed down in his family for generations.

He filled the glass of water on his altar to the brim saying, "for the ancestors on whose shoulders I stand," while staring reverently at the photographs of deceased relatives placed there alongside his mother's urn of ashes. Eric carefully named all the dead relatives he could remember, and then followed up by acknowledging "all other ancestors known to me and unknown." He tore the slice of bread he'd brought in half, laying one piece on the offering plate in front of him and slowly chewing on the other piece.

As he closed his eyes, Eric let the taste of the bread take him back to his childhood memories, standing in the kitchen with his grandmother and great-grandmother as they sang songs and prepared the family dinner together. A smile crept across his lips as he smelled baking bread and could hear the laughter and music in his memory. He let the feelings from his memory rest on his mind like a lizard basking on a rock, and enjoyed the moment without any hurry.

Eric's ancestors had arrived. The sickly sweet smell of his grandfather's cigars seemed to burn the inside of his nostrils. At that moment, Eric knew his beloved dead were with him and that the only difference was that he couldn't give them a physical hug anymore. They were there still, ready to help him. He opened his eyes and began to pray in thanks to his ancestors, asking them for their aid as he reached for his divination tools to begin to work. Eric is a psychic who uses the senses of smell and taste in his psychic work.

They say that scent is the strongest sense tied to memory. Perhaps this is why it is one of the senses that often tells psychic mediums that a deceased person is present. For example, when my dearly departed dad visits my psychic mom who is still living, she often can smell his cigarette smoke. I, on the other hand, tend to smell his Old Spice aftershave, probably because he knows how strongly I disliked his smoking when he was alive.

Clairsalient and Clairgustant Exercises

If you tend to notice smells that aren't really there, that might be a good indicator that you have this psychic sense, which can be used to confirm and identify the presence of an entity that you can use as a source of your psychic information. Begin to note these sensations during your meditations. Experiencing a taste in your mouth during psychic work can happen, though it may be significantly more rare. However, taste can still play an important role in connecting people during psychic work. Eating a meal that reminds you of a person, living or dead, before or after a telepathy or mediumship session can quickly take you there. Eating food can also be very grounding, so it can be the perfect end to a particularly intense reading.

In many cultures, food offerings are given to or shared with the dead. A good Samhain or Halloween ritual for the budding psychic medium is to hold a dumb supper. A dumb supper is a Pagan practice in which a person or group of people bring food their ancestors or beloved dead people would have enjoyed, and eat it in silence while thinking about the deceased. Photographs of those who have passed can be around the table or at its center, and small offerings or libations may be placed out on a plate for them to enjoy before they are discarded outdoors. A dumb supper can be a very moving and powerful experience, and can show any deceased people who are your sources of psychic information how much you appreciate them in order to encourage them to keep helping you in the future.

The best times for a dumb supper are near Samhain, (Halloween), or during the dark phase of the moon. Make sure each guest is comfortable with the idea of divination tools and communing with their own dead loved ones before inviting them. Have each guest bring photographs of deceased family members. The photographs should not have any living people in them. For a traditional dumb supper, loved ones who are not related or pets should not be used.

Each guest should also bring a potluck dish. Hopefully, this can be a dish that their deceased family member would have loved. If the ancestors in question were never known to the guest while in life, have the guest bring a dish appropriate to the nationality or region of their ancestors. Divination tools should be made available for guests, even if they're as simple as a dark bowl filled with water, a bowl of milk, or a lit candle for scrying.

A somber tone should be set with the decorations to prepare everyone for serious work. The space can be lit with candles and the photographs placed in the center of the table. A decorative plate can be set out to place offerings and glasses of water to honor the ancestors. When it is time for the supper to begin, the space is arranged and the guests are seated. A small portion of each dish should be placed on the offering plate before anyone eats.

Brief everyone ahead of time that the supper should be consumed silently in order to facilitate meditation, without interaction between you and your guests or the guests with each other. If you wish, set times for the start and end of the silent period, or just go with the flow. In contrast to a séance in which the psychic medium is in charge and acting as the middle man between the deceased and the living, a dumb supper is a community event that provides personal and intimate meditative moments for the people involved to commune directly with their beloved dead.

After the meal has been finished, the contents of the offering plate should be left outdoors. You and the guests may choose to converse about any personal experiences or revelations that occurred during the course of their personal meditations. Since the dumb supper is far more private an experience than a séance, nobody should be pressured to share his or her feelings if it does not feel right to do so.

....

Homework

Solo

Think about what form of these two learning styles you tend to use best: visual or auditory. Follow the advice to develop your talents with that sense, starting with the one that you find is your most natural learning style. Then, use the advice for developing the other two senses associated with the learning styles that are not your best.

For example, if you are a visual learner, pick a form of scrying divination, and get started as a clairvoyant psychic, while working on meditating with white noise in the morning or evening to improve your clairaudience. If you are an auditory learner, jump straight into listening during your meditations in order to find answers to questions as a clairaudient psychic, but work on your clairvoyance by practicing visualizations before or afterward.

Whether or not you are a body-kinesthetic learner, use the technique based on *Delsarte System of Expression*. It can be used in order to both get more in tune with your body if you're a little clueless, or start making a coordinated effort at making sense of psychic messages from your body, if you're a little more self-aware. As I mentioned, you might be able to jump in to practice using your body as a pendulum, swaying back and forth or in a circle depending on the answers to your questions. You'll have to ask yourself what means "yes" and what means "no" before you get started. However, the idea behind Delsarte's system is that each part of your body relates to a specific area of focus, and sensations can draw your attention to these. Jump to the section on clairtangent exercises to try out the beginner's exercise with Delsarte's system.

With a Partner

As soon as you've got a willing partner, it is a good idea to practice your chosen form of divination with him or her as your pretend client. Divination is a fine tool for personal practice, but it is interesting to see how your interpretations change or don't change when you are working with your expectations, or lack thereof, of a partner. Take note of any point in the reading in which you did not communicate as clearly, or were incorrect in your assumptions, and pay attention to how your technique or your style may have differed from solo practice with your divination tools.

If you tend towards having clairvoyant skills during your solo homework, expand by trying to see auras with a partner and becoming familiar with what poses might mean in Delsarte's system of expression, as described in the clairvoyant exercises. By now, you've hopefully practiced the meditation based on Delsarte's system of expression on your own. Push yourself to feel auras as well, by trying out the clairtangent exercise of mirroring your partner. In order to practice with your senses of smell and taste, I suggest holding a dumb supper with like-minded people.

2 Techniques

When I was five years old, I marched into my first piano lesson with confidence written all over my small face. "I already know how to play the piano," I announced to my instructor's raised eyebrows. I climbed up onto the seat in front of the huge instrument, raised my arms high over my head just like the pianists I had seen in cartoons, closed my eyes, and tossed my hair back before slamming my fingers down on the keys. The cacophony I created elicited laughter from all the adults in the room, but I was confused. Surely, I believed, my passion and drive meant that I would automatically have the skills to match. Of course I could literally play the piano, since depressing the keys did not require any special abilities, but I did not yet know the techniques of how to make beautiful music or the harmonious sounds I wanted to make.

Techniques to help you focus
and bring out your psychic abilities

Psychic abilities naturally exist in everyone, just as music can naturally exist everywhere in the universe. But like the little girl at the piano who couldn't play a concerto in the opening example, you won't be able to use your talents in order to help yourself and others if you do not diligently learn and practice techniques to develop, nurture, and focus your psychic abilities. This chapter has several techniques that will allow your psychic abilities to work in concert with your will.

Journal

The most important tool for a beginning psychic—more important than any divination tool—is a journal. Without a journal, tracking your progress cannot be done with any degree of accuracy. You might accidentally fudge your memory in favor of your psychic abilities or, more likely, you will dismiss a prediction as inaccurate and then never realize later on that it was actually spot-on when it finally came to pass. Disciplining yourself to keep a journal may be extremely difficult, but starting the habit early in your practice will not only make you a better psychic, it will give you a way to constantly and consistently work to improve your practice.

When procuring a journal, it may be tempting to buy or make one that looks mystical or beautiful. I suggest looking for a utilitarian three-ring binder. If looks matter to you, decorate it. Avoiding bound books is helpful because they are not often very helpful for organizing your work chronologically. Dating your entries is important for finding out if there are patterns between when your predictions occur and when they come to pass. However, keeping everything in order by date simply makes it less likely that you're going to read through every page in the past in order to land on useful information. Keep a binder or file folder with pages you can move and reorganize, in order to make sure that things you write down aren't tucked away, never to see the light of day again.

How you organize your journal depends greatly on the type of work you choose to do as a psychic, hence the usefulness of a journal you can reorganize on a whim. That being said, I suggest organizing it by symbolic meanings at first. When you begin receiving psychic messages, many of them won't be literal. They may be steeped in a language of your own subconscious symbolism. Your brain receives riddles instead of clear messages because the intuitive part of your brain, like the part of your brain that dreams, does not speak in words and logic but rather through pictures or symbolism. For example, if you see the image of your house on fire in a psychic message, it doesn't necessarily mean that your house is actually going to burn down. Seeing a house on fire may mean that your home will undergo a transformation, showing you that you might move to a new home. Or, in an even more symbolically abstract way, the home might represent your sense of stability needing to undergo a change.

If you begin to organize the things you perceive alphabetically by name, you will be able to create your own personal psychic dictionary. Alphabetizing is useful not only to speed up your ability to interpret a particularly cryptic message, but also to track how your interpretations change over time. For example, when you were a child, symbols of autumn may have strongly been associated with going back to school, and thus pointed you to messages about learning and study. As an adult, the fall may be more associated with things coming to an end. Refusing to acknowledge the natural shift of the meanings of your symbols over time might make your readings become more confusing or less accurate.

Sharing your journal may be tempting, especially if you already openly share many parts of your life with others on the Internet, for example. I am a very public person myself but I suggest you keep your psychic journal just to yourself, especially at first. If you share with others, even if you are an honest and open person, you may find that you censor yourself a little bit. For example, if you have a vision that is highly sexual or violent in nature, or you find yourself making a prediction that is highly unlikely to come to pass, you might allow yourself to forget about it before recording it or omit pieces that are important to your development of your understanding of the message's meaning.

Just because you aren't organizing your journal chronologically doesn't mean that you shouldn't write in it every day. Set aside some time for yourself to write in your journal daily. Your quiet time should be undisturbed and at a point during your day when you usually feel clear-headed and have some energy and mental attention to finish this task properly. Since this isn't simply a log of your thoughts, I understand if you don't have any psychic things to write every day. Set aside time anyway for yourself. Otherwise, when you do have important things to write, you may not have the routine time built into your schedule to properly give them the attention they deserve. If you have nothing to write on a given day, you can simply add that time to the total you have set aside for quiet meditation.

If you pride yourself in having nothing to hide, as I do, go ahead and share some of your work openly if that is your desire but allow yourself a special place to put those thoughts and feelings you don't choose to share. Giving yourself privacy is not deceptive. Rarely is one required to say everything he or she thinks, and if a person does say everything that crosses his or her mind, that person is more likely to be perceived as a fool than someone noted for their honesty.

What should you write in your journal? Each psychic reading you do might lead to small, short entries on multiple pages of your journal as you break it apart into the different predictions and different symbols you may have experienced. If predictions already tend to spring to your mind, begin recording these immediately no matter how silly or unlikely they might seem. Remember, they may be symbolic and their meaning might become more clear to you later, once the actual event has taken place. If you have pictures or words spring to mind during meditation that seem significant to you, go ahead and record those as well. Most importantly, you should immediately begin breaking apart and recording the symbols in your dreams.

Grounding

Have you ever had a task ahead of you that required concentration but you felt entirely in the wrong head-space to be able to complete it? Imagine for example you are a student needing to sit down and study for an important exam the following day. But instead of feeling ready to open your textbook, you feel jittery and agitated. You might feel more like doing jumping jacks than sitting still and thinking clearly. Maybe you have a whopping headache or the kind of fatigue that clouds your thinking. In such a case you would be what I refer to as "ungrounded," and you may need to perform grounding exercises in order to feel both relaxed and alert.

Grounding, then, is mental or physical action you can take to affect your energetic state to become more relaxed and focused. Energy in this case does not refer directly to the literal metabolic, chemical energy in your body but the more metaphorical and spiritual chi, the flow of which you can direct with your will in order to manifest things in your life. If chi is sufficient and flowing well, you will be able to undertake tasks that require a lot of effort and concentration such as running a marathon or planning a wedding. But if your chi is reduced in some way or is blocked so as to become stagnant, you will not be able to muster much more than the gumption required to hit the snooze button on your alarm and call in sick to work.

As you might imagine, grounding is a useful skill not only for psychics but for everyone, especially those who have high-stress jobs or who live in a chaotic household. When I worked as a middle school and high school teacher, I came to be thankful every day that I was highly skilled in grounding methods. In fact, I believe that not being able to either deflect or harmlessly ground the intense energies of adolescents is why many teachers burn out quickly. Teenagers are highly emotional and much of their extremes of love or hatred are projected onto those around them. I believe that successful teachers of such kids who weren't explicitly trained in grounding techniques must have subconsciously learned them as a survival tactic.

Being able to instantly rein in your own feelings of frenetic energy and direct it towards quieter pursuits is something every person should attempt with their bodies and minds. Calming down is something we all try to do naturally, so perhaps you've already developed coping mechanisms such as petting your cat or going for a jog. Relaxing activities you already do are perfectly fine coping aids, so continue to use them during this process. However,

I will give you a few more tools to use when attempting to ground yourself; please try them out. If you already have a method that works better, please don't hesitate to continue using it instead.

Relaxation can be achieved through all of your senses, just as psychic perceptions can come through all of them as well. I will give you some examples of grounding activities you can try with each of them. Some of them can be combined more easily than others but please try them individually before you begin to combine them. The reason that one method doesn't work the same way all the time is because some days you may be more ungrounded than others and you may need to pull out another option from your toolbox to combat this feeling. You should be able to appropriately meet your needs with your actions.

The sight of something relaxing can instantly relieve feelings of excess, jittery energy. If you are able to visualize relaxing scenery, this may be your first resource. You may find that simply using a darkened room, candles, or soft lighting does the trick for you. Some imagine themselves to be a tree in the woods safely drawing up energy from the earth that can be used for the task at hand, and pushing excess energy back into it to be harmlessly dispersed. If you find it difficult to imagine visual scenes, you may consider staring at a picture of peaceful scenery. You can buy a painting, or even make a collage of woodland views. When I was a college student, I pasted pictures of sunsets, mountains, trees, and lakes onto the inside of a file folder I could prop up at my work station when I studied in the library.

Sound is often a powerful relaxer, so prepare yourself a selection of songs or ambient white noise that you find relaxing, such as nature sounds. Rather than having a great deal of variety as you might prefer for entertainment, you may find that repetition of the same familiar sounds is helpful while grounding. As your body and mind become used to settling down to business each time you hear those particular sounds, you may find them to be instant keys to producing those results when you condition yourself to them time and time again.

Your sense of smell can more easily condition you into a specific state of mind as it is the sense most closely tied to memory. The study of aromatherapy can guide you to many scents that can produce amazing results but it is so vast that it is beyond the scope of this book. However, you may find that a specific scent (such as lavender) relaxes you. If you land on a specific essential oil or perfume that works for you and use it only during times when you work to make yourself feel grounded, you'll find it to be a very handy tool to quickly move you into that state of being.

Taste can be an important sense for grounding because the act of eating is grounding in itself. Feeling jittery and overstressed is hard to do when you feel contentedly full. However, unless you want to develop an eating disorder, specific foods aren't a good crutch to get hooked on for grounding purposes. However, the use of salt for grounding has been done in many western magical circles. If you don't have reason to watch your salt intake, a tiny bit of table salt or sea salt placed on the tip of your tongue can be very grounding.

Your sense of touch can help with grounding in many ways; this physical method is most likely one you have already developed subconsciously. In fact, some people have learned to ground themselves simply by being in proximity to other people who are more relaxed than they are. Such people are often dubbed "psychic vampires" because they can unbalance your own relaxed state by using you in order to feel more comfortable themselves. Have you ever felt mentally and emotionally drained after having a conversation with somebody who seemed to be chaotic and stressed or manipulative? Your tiring confrontation might have been an encounter with such a psychic vampire. You can avoid becoming one yourself by focusing on calming yourself through physiological means while alone, or at least alone in the beginning.

Touching the earth or a rock can be of help when grounding—some psychics carry a piece of hematite with them for exactly this purpose. Removing your shoes and socks and connecting barefoot with the ground can be a physical link and a cue that is highly effective for grounding. Exercise can be a good method for grounding. For some, a good jog can be a repetitive and meditative way to even out moods and energies. For others, dancing can be a grounding experience. As an example, some Arabic cultures dance the *zaar* as a healing way to expunge a person of a malicious djinn (genie). Got some bad energies inside you? Dance them out!

After grounding, it is often useful to center yourself. Centering is the act of settling your mind into this place, this time, and the task at hand. One way to center yourself is to begin by just observing your place in the room or wherever you might be. For example, if you are in the bedroom of an apartment, think about where you are located in that room, sitting on the bed perhaps. Then, imagine that room's relationship to the other rooms in the home, such as the kitchen and the bathroom. Next think about all the other apartments above, below, and to the sides. Think about the many floors below and the firm earth beneath the building. Imagine where you are situated in your town, state, and country. Finally, think about your place on the earth and in the universe. After this visualization, you may feel more humble and small but you may also find yourself more centered and connected with the moment.

Meditation

There are two components to any conversation. One is speaking your mind, in one way or another, even if you happen to be using sign language. The other is listening to what the other person has to say. When you want to be a psychic perceiving information from a paranormal source, you'll need to give time to perceive or "listen" to that information. The ideal way to do this is through the practice of meditation. If you take time out of the daily noise and buzz of everyday life to simply sit in a receptive state, you'll instantly have more of a two-sided conversation with that supernatural source of information. At the very least you'll enjoy the stress-relieving effects that relaxing meditation has to offer.

If you are unfamiliar or unpracticed with meditation, don't worry, and certainly don't avoid getting started. As a kid, I was diagnosed with Attention Deficit Hyperactivity Disorder and started out with the focus and attention span of a gnat. If I can do it, anyone can. I put off starting my own personal spiritual meditation as a child and teenager because I thought it was boring to sit there without thoughts in my head. In order to have controlled meditation however, this silent and receptive state is just the way you'll need to be. Using guided meditations busy with imagery may be less difficult, but you'll bring more peace and power to your own mind if you can start with a "blank slate" and let that supernatural source fill it with information. Thinking about "nothing" is better for clearing purposes than trying to imagine something calming or somebody else's ideas (however interesting) for guided meditation. Guided meditations can be limiting for a beginner, so start with quiet receptive meditation and move on to create your own visualizations later if desired.

So how do you get started with meditation? Begin by trying to find a quiet place with very few distractions, like a room in your house with a locked door, for example.

Unplug the phone and turn off your cell, your smartphone, or pager. Take your meditation environment seriously and don't just wave away the need to unplug phones and eliminate all other distractions. The more excuses you give yourself to get up and walk away from your meditation, the less effective and the more like a chore this routine will be. You need to create a sanctuary.

Most books and teachers say to start with a small amount of time such as five minutes and work up from there. I wholeheartedly endorse this, because if you start with a very long meditation, you may feel frustrated quickly. Give yourself small successes at first. In fact, I think five minutes is an awfully long time for the absolute beginner to clear his or her mind. I'd say you're a winner if you can push out all your own thoughts for even thirty seconds in the beginning. It might be a stretch at first, so don't move on to longer blocks of time—even one minute longer—until you've mastered many shorter attempts. Think of meditation as a preparing for a marathon, not a sprint. Silent meditation is something for which you must train your mind and it is not a state you can just turn on and off when you first begin.

Once you've taken this seriously and have locked the door after the kids and husband are out of the house and disconnected all your communication gadgets, how do you get started? Your brain doesn't have an off switch. Quieting your mind may take some preparation at first before you can undertake the task of meditation. Start out by attempting to relax. Creating a calming environment might involve dimming the lights, lighting some candles, putting on some relaxing music or the sounds of nature, and getting into a comfortable seated or lying position. Stretch your muscles or try the technique of tensing each of them and relaxing them one at a time starting with your toes and working your way up your body. Slowing your breathing and listening to your body can be both an effective way to relax and a method of focusing on something other than your racing thoughts to try to clear your mind.

I like to begin by listening to and feeling my own heartbeat and breathing as it exists naturally after my grounding and before my meditation. You can use the method of "square breathing." Square breathing is a method of controlling and slowing your breathing in order to relax and focus. Breathe in for four counts, hold your breath for four counts, breathe out for four counts, and then hold for four more before repeating the cycle. For new students, this can be challenging and even a barrier to meditation, often because the counts are done so slowly. Working with periods of time measured in seconds, most beginners try to use counts that are one second long. Counting so slowly can work, but there can be quite a physiological whiplash if you try to slow your breathing to one second counts directly from breathing quick and shallow breaths. Running up the stairs, plopping down in your chair, and diving straight into slow and square breathing may result in failure.

Instead, use your heart rate as a guide for how long the counts should be. Use four heartbeats to a count. So if your heart rate is still pretty high from a stressful day, or from physical activity, your four beats will last a shorter duration, and your square breathing will be slightly faster. As you start and continue the square breathing to your heart beat, you will notice the rate gradually slow at your body's own pace as you relax. Let your body set this pace and go with it, even if you feel like you're not calming down as quickly as you would like. With practice, this time will improve for you.

In order to slow your breathing in a healthy and calming way, breathe deeply using your diaphragm rather than trying to control the speed using your throat or your chest. You can do this by first allowing your shoulders to relax, placing your hand on your navel, and breathing deep enough so that your belly rises slowly outward while your shoulders and chest stay relaxed. Deep breathing allows you to fill your lungs to a greater capacity with fresh air as well as to modulate your breathing more calmly and regularly.

At this point, you should be able to relax yourself at least somewhat relative to your normal alert and active state. You may transition to clearing your mind by continuing at first to focus on your internal cues such as your heartbeat and your breathing. Whenever your mind wanders away to what might be happening elsewhere or what you have to do later on in the day, gently bring your focus back to your breathing or heartbeat without reprimanding yourself. As thoughts surface, try to observe them passively, as if they belong to somebody else. Let them float away without following up with further consideration. If this seems like a tall order, remember to just start out with thirty seconds and then relax again and allow yourself to think freely. You may wish to write down any mundane thoughts like "pick up more juice from the store" that came up so you won't have to worry about them anymore, and then try again. With daily practice, you may learn to write down those "to do" thoughts before you begin attempting to meditate so they don't interfere.

Why should you practice meditation frequently, even if you don't want to have a psychic session every day? Well first of all, it is very good for you. Taking a break with meditation can help to lower your stress, and this "time-out" can be as physically refreshing as a nap or a healthy meal. You may also find that your cognitive abilities and memory drastically improve after meditation. If you want to be a psychic, you must be well-practiced in meditation so you can call up this state at a moment's notice rather than having to run through all the preparation and exercises outlined above. You don't have time for a learning curve, and you have a lot of work ahead of you during an actual reading. Meditation is not just a tool in your kit—it is a vital component of being a psychic that you'll want to be able to access naturally and quickly without having to think about it.

MEDITATION VISUALIZATION EXERCISES

In order to practice visualization, I suggest you start simply with an object. A good homework object for you would be your favorite fruit. Take it with you into your meditation room, and take a few minutes after grounding and centering but before meditation to study everything about it. Feel its size and weight in your hands, smell it, and visually inspect it thoroughly. Set the fruit down in front of you, and begin your meditation.

Close your eyes and visualize every aspect of the fruit, including the color, size, and texture. Imagine holding your hands out in front of you (but don't actually do so). In your mind, feel the fruit's skin. Feel the weight press into your palms, cool to the touch and warming with your skin contact. Turn the fruit in your imaginary hands and explore it with your mind. Smell the scent and then in your mind's eye, eat the fruit. Feel the crunch of it on your teeth and the juices in your mouth. Chew and swallow in your visualization until the entire virtual fruit has been devoured. The meditation should be a pleasant experience.

You can perform this exercise frequently. You can even imagine the fruit is imbued with a quality you wish to have, such as healing energy or a calm sense of peace. Using this visualization, you can make those energies a part of you with something simple as a piece of fruit. You can try visualizing other objects as well for practice. You'll find that things which were once living and things which were never living have a different sense about them when held in your mind. Try this out so that later, you'll be able to sense this when you receive psychic messages about non-living things. Finally, round out your object visualization by using a living object such as a plant or a pet.

Once you've mastered simple and complex objects, you can work on visualizing entire spaces. Begin with the room in which you are meditating. After grounding and centering but before meditation, study the room carefully. As with the fruit exercise, explore the room with as many of your senses as possible (though there may not be anything edible present). Look at the objects in the room, being careful to note colors and numbers of things. Touch as many surfaces as possible, feeling the texture and temperature of each one. As you begin to meditate, take note of any scents you can smell and sounds you can hear before concentrating on quiet receptivity.

After you've established your silent meditation, you can begin to work on reconstructing the entire room in your mind's eye. Complete visualization is considerably more complex than simply trying to recall all of the objects in the room. Work hard to recreate everything about the room in your mind, so you can imagine walking around it and interacting with anything you wish. You are working out your visualization skills as well as creating this space in a spiritual form on the astral plane. The astral plane is a spiritual space where you can go to meet spiritual beings or look for messages from those supernatural sources, very much like an alternate dimension.

When you are able to call up the room you occupy during meditation, you can branch out to calling to mind a familiar space in which you are not currently located, like another room in the house. If you can do that well enough, you may wish to work on creating a space in your mind's eye that does not yet exist. You can make this your ideal place with all your favorite smells, colors, and objects. Don't put people or other living creatures in there just yet, as you'll want to be able to invite whomever you wish to enter this special place of yours. Allow this space to be a relaxing retreat when you need it. The sacred place you have just created is your home base; it is a protected place where nothing can harm you. Nothing can enter without your permission, and it is there to aid you whenever you wish. Practice until you can go to your sacred place in an instant.

Guided meditations are often a fun way to make your meditations more entertaining and work on your visualization skills. Grab a partner. Have him or her practice the object and place meditations described in the solo homework assignment. Practice quietly meditating together as you both recreate the room that you occupy in your own minds. Next, give yourselves a few more minutes to recreate another space with which you both are familiar, such as a favorite coffee shop you both frequent.

After this, each of you can take turns creating a space in your mind that exists but that your partner may have not yet visited, such as the living room of a favorite relative. As you take your turn and visualize such a space, describe it aloud to your partner so he or she can imagine it as well. Putting words to what you see not only builds your observation skills, but your ability to communicate the things that you visualize, which is a vital skill for psychic readings. When each of you has had a turn describing a real place, try an astral place. If you feel comfortable sharing your personal ideal space you have created, invite your partner into that space and help create it in his or her mind as you do so. Sit quietly after you have done so and allow yourselves to commune with each other on the astral plane. You may find that you are able to connect in new psychic ways.

Dreams

If I had to name one thing that each person could do in order to improve or become in tune with their own psychic abilities, it would be to pay attention to dreams. Rather than requiring a divination system to learn, dreams are something with which we each have experience. In addition, the difficult challenge of noting the difference between the real and the unreal can be laid aside in dream analysis. One can assume that nothing in a dream is literally "real" yet still gain a lot of interesting information from it.

Ideally, being psychic should be like swimming in the ocean. You can stay on dry land or paddle to keep your head above the water in the real world, or hold your breath to dive below to experience another world entirely. Dreaming is like being temporarily fully submerged in that strange other world. You can learn what your inner mind has for you in the way of symbolism so that you can better recognize them when those things speak to you in your waking life. Interpreting symbols is sort of like learning another language; full immersion in its country of origin would be ideal. Dive into your own subconscious to find out where your psychic inklings originate.

When I first started keeping track of my dreams, I found it extremely challenging to remember and record them. I found that the moment I awoke the dreams began to flee from my memory such that if I delayed even long enough to use the bathroom, they would be entirely forgotten. Even when the dream was so odd I'd think to myself, "Surely I will remember this later; I can go back to sleep for now," it would be completely gone by the time I was at my computer or piece of paper ready to write about it. In this case, it may be helpful to have a separate dream journal kept by your bed for recording them in a narrative style before picking them apart for your psychic journal.

Make it a discipline to write in your dream journal the instant you wake up before doing anything else—even getting a drink of water or heading to the toilet. Have a small flashlight by your bed if you have a significant other you do not wish to disturb. Keeping a dream journal can be extremely challenging but rewarding if you treat it as a serious spiritual or personal discipline you need to master. After a while, it will be second nature and won't seem like such a chore to fight yourself awake to write. In fact, you'll find things written down that you don't even remember writing since you will have done it while in that alpha wave state between sleep and wakefulness.

On a semi-regular basis, say once a month, I'd recommend going through your dream journal and taking some things from it to add to your psychic journal. I recommend circling things that might be symbols such as important nouns or verbs. Pay special attention if a person, place, thing, or action is repeated in your dreams multiple times in a week. Add these recurrences to your psychic journal along with your guess about possible interpretations if you have any.

If you had a precognitive dream—that is, something you dreamed later came true in real life—highlight it with a pen and record it near the appropriate symbols along with the date you had the dream and the date that it actually came to pass. You may notice a pattern begins to form whenever you see certain things in your dreams that tip you off to their significance in your waking life. My mother, who often has quite prophetic dreams, noticed when a plane crash happened in the news seven days after one in her dream with the exact same details. From this experience, she came to realize that many of her precognitive dreams foretell events that occur a week later. Read through those dreams again once or twice a year to see if any more have come true that simply took more time to happen.

I know that reading through something that you've already written can be boring. Indeed, I loathe the process of revising my books, even though I love writing them. A good way to evoke emotion in your stale dream journal entries is to get creative by drawing pictures, making a collage, or writing a poem.

DREAM ANALYSIS STEP-BY-STEP

1. Write down your dreams the moment you awaken, even if going back to sleep afterward. Date each entry carefully so you know what night you had each dream.

2. Revisit your dream journal regularly. Try doing it whenever you set your clocks forward or back. Remember when you're setting your clock to "look back in time" at your dreams. When you analyze your dreams, do so right before bed so that you can encourage your brain to dream about the same subject matter again.

3. When looking at a dream, first make sure you circle any words that may be a symbol. Every noun that you wrote in your dream journal might be a symbol.

4. Highlight any sentences in the dream that later literally came true. Dreams that tell the future are precognitive.

5. Right before bed, rekindle and recapture the emotions in one of your dreams that seemed either precognitive or full of symbolic nouns or passionate subject matter. Since the right hemisphere of your brain is the brain

structure that dreams as well as creates, make something artistic. Draw or paint your dream, or write a poem that makes you feel emotional when you read it aloud.

6. Go to sleep immediately after creating something from your dream, and take care to write down any further dreams that you have. Make a note by these new entries to look back at the entry that you were analyzing deeply and creatively right before bed.

Here is an example of dream journal work that my mother (her name is Jean) created in order to start puzzling out why she tends to have dreams about accidents. As you read through her later analysis, think about how you would begin to start understanding your own dreams. Even if you cannot interpret them at the time, you can ask important questions that can help you understand how you dream. She advises my readers at the time of this writing to pay attention to whether dream events that you have experienced happen to other people around you, or are simply related to events that you yourself tend to see later on in the news or in your real waking life.

On May 4, 2010, Jean had a dream about a terrible train crash she found very disturbing, but she wrote some notes about it in her dream journal. On May 10, 2010, the story broke in the *Edmonton Sun* that three people died after a train collided with a truck. She was shaken by the news—the photograph of the twisted wreckage was so evocative of her dream imagery that she realized the dream had been precognitive. As she looked at the photographs of two little girls who had died, she agonized over her wish that she could have somehow prevented the crash because she had known ahead of time that it was going to happen, but of course that was impossible. So moved was Jean by this experience, that she wrote the following poem about that dream journal entry six months later.

DREAM JOURNAL—MAY 4, 2010

all the color has been washed out of the scene
a locomotive is approaching, shoveling a wave
    of snow ahead of it
the moving picture rendered in blacks and
    whites and grays
an embroidered veil of snow screens the view
drifting softly silent
I'm standing right here
to the right of the track
watching the train approach
not feeling the cold
but I am here

for some reason I can't hear the chugging
    of the engine
or feel the vibration under my feet
but I am here
then everything happens so fast

a gray truck whizzes by from the right
it crumples against the solid steel plow
    of the engine
no sound

then motion stops and the truck
now a jagged and flattened piece of metal
is stuck there like a bug on a windscreen

I wake up

watching the news at noon I see the
    train again
rendered in black and white and gray
a blizzard blows a slanted static of
    snow over everything
and here comes the train
just as I had remembered it
chugging slowly toward the camera
pushing snow ahead of it

a reporter looks into the camera
in a box in the upper corner of the screen
a tangled chunk of metal lies in a ditch
it looks cold and lonely
he describes what happened that morning

snow had hammered Edmonton
and at 8:40 AM

a local man had somehow driven his Silverado
    under the arms of the warning gate the
    flashing lights had been either obscured
    by the blizzard
or ignored by the man
and the truck had been crushed by a passing
    Via Rail train
his two little girls had died with him
two engineers had asked to be relieved of duty
    for the day.

I turn off the news and put another post it
    note in my dream journal
I had written on it in shaky hand the date and
    the details of the accident.

As Jean wrote the poem, working through the symbolism and the imagery helped her connect the images she saw with the emotions she felt. The next day, upon switching on the television to watch the news, to her horror she saw another image of twisted metal that jarred her with the memory of that dream and of the visions that moved through her head as she had written that poem. She quickly added underneath her poem in her dream journal the following addition to the entry: "Written Nov 19, 2010 at 9:30 PM by Jean Pawlucki. Nov. 20, 2010, at 8:15 AM, a flagger in Langley was injured in her truck when it was pushed by a slow moving train 30 feet. I didn't dream of it, but why did I write the poem last night?"

While writing her poem about the accident in May, she entered a meditative state that made her quite receptive to symbolism that would point to the November accident that would take place the following day. In this way, precognitive dreams can be used as a meditation tool in order to increase your psychic ability in your waking life. Jean still asks questions about why she dreams or writes the things she does at the times that they occur, and by doing so, she's able to begin to learn a little bit more about her psychic self. Be sure to always write down the dates and times of not only your dreams but your analyses of them as well. Don't be afraid to ask hard questions about the visions you see. You may have a reason for the psychic learning path you've chosen, and there may be a purpose behind even the most horrible of realizations.

You can even begin to use your dreams to attempt to answer questions or solve problems. Before you go to bed, ground yourself and meditate on a question you would like answered in your dreams or a problem with several scenarios played out in your dreams. Record the results, even if you think it was a failed attempt. Some symbolic dreams don't make sense right away but may make perfect sense later on. You might even wish to ask for a deceased family member or friend to appear in a dream. Experiencing time with a loved one again in this manner can be very rewarding, and he or she may be able to help you with a problem or give you information.

Developing greater control over your dreams can help you to use them as a problem-solving tool, as some psychologists believe this is the ultimate natural purpose of dreaming anyway. At the very least, gaining this confidence can help you change the direction of your dreams should they become unpleasant. Eventually you'll need not suffer nightmares very often if you happen to be prone to bad dreams.

How To Dream With Someone

Find a friend who is just as interested in psychic development as you, or who at least is willing to give permission for you to work together through your dreams. Ideally, each of you will meditate before bed to try to visit each other during your dreams. Time is a very strange thing in your dreams; you may have noticed it can seem like days, months, or even years pass in a dream when it can't have been more than one night's sleep. In reality, dream time accounts for mere seconds of the Rapid Eye Movement stage of sleep. You don't have to be sleeping and dreaming at the very same instant in time but if you want to synchronize your sleeping and waking hours to hedge your bets, you may.

Make sure your partner knows to write down dreams the instant he or she wakes up. You may need to try this exercise several nights before it works. Some find that connecting with others in dreams is easier to do during the full moon. Once you've mastered this technique with a partner, it can be extremely useful when you need to be physically distant from a family member or a loved one for some time. For an example of two people dreaming together, read chapter 5's section on telepathy. Experiencing a shared dream together can feel much more fulfilling than a telephone call as a way to connect and be emotionally close.

After having practiced with a real live person, you may wish to attempt dreaming with a deceased ancestor. As amazing as it is to connect with a living person over a distance, I can't put into words what a blessing it can be to hug a dearly departed loved one again in a dream. You can connect with deceased people who are willing simply by thinking about them before bed, asking them in your mind to appear, or by praying for a connection with your deceased loved one. I find that if I simply say aloud to those ancestors who are around me and guarding me that I welcome them in my dreams and that their presence in my dreaming won't frighten me, my loved ones do indeed come. After inviting an ancestor to your dreams, it is polite to allow them to lead the topics of conversation, especially when you are new to the process.

I remember recently after my father died, that all he'd wanted to talk about were practical issues. He was a medal collector, and when he would appear in my dreams he would frantically explain to me things that had to be done. For example, a Russian medal group had to be paired with some documents in order for it to be sold at proper value. He would give me detailed and complicated instructions, and when I awoke I would be exhausted. When I recorded my dreams in my dream journal, I felt like a court reporter, hurriedly writing all of the pertinent instructional information down before it fled from memory.

After a while, the character of my dreams with my father changed. Now when he comes to my dreams, he brings simple messages of love or warm advice for the deeper matters in my life like my marriage and family. He tells me to relax and reminds me how proud he is. When I awake to record my dreams, I feel loved and write of pleasant experiences with him.

....

Homework

Solo

Chapter two has plenty of homework for you to do on your own. Procure a journal in which you can record your private psychic thoughts. I suggest a binder or a file folder so you can rearrange pieces of paper at will. You can also get another journal that can be bound in any manner in which you can record your dreams in a more narrative style. Begin recording any premonitions you have and any symbolic dream messages. Set aside time daily in which to write, even if some days you don't have anything to record.

Begin practicing grounding frequently. You may find that it is helpful before or after you go to work at your job as well as before meditation, writing in your journals, and bedtime. Begin practicing meditation daily, even if it is just a thirty-second long attempt after grounding. When you feel comfortable with silent, receptive meditation, you can begin visualizations.

I must stress that you should force yourself not to skip the boring meditations without visualization, as that is the most important state for psychic work. However, visualization can be a good skill to exercise, especially when you begin receiving visual perceptions during meditation. The more you attempt visualizations during meditation, the longer you may be able to hold those images in your mind's eye and the more details you may be able to pick up.

With a Partner

As I mentioned, beginning with your dreams is a good place to start doing very interesting psychic work, because everybody already dreams. Find a willing partner who would like to increase his or her psychic skills and try dreaming together. Look for instructions on how to dream with someone in the dreams section of this chapter. Becoming skilled with this can be fun and fascinating and can help you become practiced enough to invite other beings into your dreams later on, such as described in the following chapter.

Another fun way to work with a partner is to perform guided meditations. Guided meditation can be done by yourself by recording your voice, but I find it much more fun and engaging if a partner is speaking aloud to me in the moment. Having a partner describe his or her own inner landscape also allows you to have your mind's eye create somebody else's visions instead of just your own. Being able to picture things you can't just imagine on your own is important for receiving psychic messages from others.

3 Who Are You Talking To?

Psychics perform the incredible task of speaking with people and beings not present with them. Such an amazing feat is like magic and can be as astounding as the first telephones must have seemed to people in the past. Have your astounding conversations with gods, ghosts, and people carefully: when you choose to have a conversation with somebody, you need to know with whom you are speaking so you can properly address them in order to be heard. If you are talking on the telephone, you need to know the right phone number as well as the procedure for speaking into the handset. If you are speaking to an audience from a stage, you need to project your voice and look around the room; a whisper over your shoulder won't be heard and you are very unlikely to get a response from your audience.

As a psychic receiving perceptions from some paranormal or supernatural source, it is important for you to consider what that source might be and make your own hypothesis so that you can start a conversation. We have not yet scientifically proven what the source may be for the information gained from psychic readings, although there are many theories. In this chapter, we will go through a few of them together and you can choose for yourself which of them may seem likely so you can attempt to address this source for yourself. Visit chapter 5 for even more ideas on communication sources. Keep in mind that perhaps only a few of them may seem true to you and that is okay. You may have another theory entirely—that's alright too.

God—Deity—Spirit

If you are a spiritual person, you may believe in a higher power such as a god or several deities. A deity might be a powerful creator either separate from or deeply connected to you. Perhaps you may identify with a great teacher such as Jesus, Muhammad, or Buddha. Maybe this higher power also takes the form of powerful entities like the *lwa* of the practice of Vodou, which are archetypes that may have once been living people, but have grown beyond that through the repeated tradition of veneration and worship projected over generations. Or, your higher power may simply be a universal concept of Spirit, a consciousness less defined than a traditional deity or collection of gods.

If you already have a spirituality or religion of your own, becoming a psychic is no reason to drop it unless your own personal journey draws you away from your current faith and into something else. In fact if you want to be a psychic and you already believe in a god or gods, chances are this practice will draw you closer to deity and cement your relationship with your life's great spiritual source.

A notable exception might be religions which specifically forbid psychic practices such as some branches of Christianity. The fact that some Christians believe psychic practices are forbidden doesn't mean that psychic work cannot be done by all Christians. There are many people who successfully blend these seemingly conflicting beliefs through a close relationship with their deity that helps them reconcile what they are doing.

This situation should not be undertaken lightly, however. If you are facing an intellectual and spiritual challenge, I encourage you to reach out to your mentors and resources. Perhaps a pastor at your church or somebody you consider a spiritual authority or peer can help you identify any conflicts and make choices or set limits accordingly. Doubt is a good thing and should not be ignored or stifled. You will either come back to your original faith stronger than ever or connect with something even better for you.

When you believe that deity is your source for information, it means that your psychic information is divine but not necessarily infallible. Even if you believe that your god or gods are omniscient, you are still a person and thus you can still make mistakes and be wrong at times.

I am often asked how accurate I am as a psychic, and I find it difficult to come up with a meaningful answer, even though they wait expectantly for it, as if it would be a percentage. But what "percentage" of the time does a human slip up in everyday life? Can you quote an accurate percentage of the times you've turned the wrong way when driving to a new location, mispronounced a word you've not yet seen before, or added a little too much sugar to your tea? We all know it has happened and it doesn't mean that you're too incompetent to drive a car, read a book, or make a decent cup of tea. Be aware of your failings as a human being, and don't let the idea of conversing with deity make you feel either too invincible or too humble to do so.

Another issue when believing deity is the source of psychic inspiration is the notion of not wanting to bother a deity with petty personal concerns. Though this may vary within and across belief systems as well, I personally like to err on the side of talking too much to the gods rather than too little. Though it may seem embarrassingly of little concern to some to bring up issues of spats with coworkers or crushes on classmates with a god, I like to side with those who believe we should always be in a state of prayer. Even when washing your dishes you can talk with deity. Each song you sing can be one to the gods. I believe that the more you speak with them, the more they listen—not the other way around. So don't be ashamed of how often you address a power greater than yourself but rather be proud of it.

If you do believe (or want to believe) that a deity is your source for psychic information, you may wish to begin your readings with a prayer in order to open the lines of communication. You can pray as if you were speaking with a friend or family member, asking for guidance in your own words and explaining the issue at hand. You can also compose or memorize a prayer to open each reading. A repeated prayer may have the added benefit of putting you in a grounded and meditative state of mind, ready to start each time you enter that frame of mind.

Below is an example of a prayer you can use to address your god or gods before a psychic reading. I find it important to ask for truth and honesty even if you are generally a very straightforward person anyway. I am very honest, but I can admit to lying to myself more than others at times...especially if I hear something I don't want to be true.

Hear my prayer, _____.
Give me the responsibility of being your psychic.
May I be open to receiving your wisdom.
Help me understand the truth, and convey it honestly.
Empower me, and those I wish to help.

Once you have performed your psychic reading, it is important to thank that higher power for helping you. Because the entity is more powerful than you, it is only prudent and polite to do so, especially if you wish to continue receiving guidance from that source. Expressing consistent gratitude to your creator can also make you feel happier about your lot in life and can bring better things to you.

I offer you my gratitude, _____.
I accept the responsibility of your message.
Your continued guidance is a blessing in my life.
I promise to use your power wisely.
Thank you for entrusting me to be your psychic.

The ritual of opening and closing your work with prayer not only has the benefit of grounding you and turning your mind toward meditation, it also establishes a relationship with deity and brings more thankfulness into your life. Ceremonial magicians believe that each time a ritual is repeated, it gains more power. Like repeated forays through the woods along the same route beat a path with your footprints, rituals leave their spiritual mark in time. The more people repeating a single ritual, the deeper its magic becomes. Everyone who reads this book and speaks these prayers aloud adds to the power of our collective work. Raise your voice with us in prayer, and you too will be a part of the power of this living history.

Your Subconscious—Your Higher Self

Imagine that you are a doubtful meditator, trying over and over again to use meditation to connect with something otherworldly, but you strongly believe you probably won't have any luck at all. You plop yourself down on the floor in your living room and squeeze your eyes shut. You push yourself to visualize a spirit guide as something amazing and fantastic to hold your attention. You make believe in your mind's eye that a bold wizard in a shiny blue robe holding a large staff appears in front of you with a burst of sparkling light. You force yourself to imagine him saying something to you. His mouth opens ominously, and he takes a deep breath. Then, in your voice, he says, "I'm just your own imagination, silly. I have nothing to say." You give up pretending you are in a deep trance state, hop up from the floor, and go watch television. Later, when a friend asks if you've ever tried meditation, you laugh and deny having ever even considered the notion.

If you happen to be a person who doesn't believe in ghosts or other spiritual entities, you might now be scoffing at people like me who want to be psychics; chiding people who believe in such things. "You're just talking to yourself," you may insist. Actually, there exists a vast source of information: a field of the subconscious or even an external field of shared subconscious information not otherwise easily accessed from our conscious minds. Talk therapy with yourself might feel more like practicing psychology than delving into the supernatural. To be frank with you, I believe that science will one day explain all our "supernatural" sources. But that doesn't mean that I think they will all turn out to be spiritual nonsense. On the contrary,

I believe the mystical world and the scientific world are not mutually exclusive.

I have to admit that there have been times in my life when I have been very skeptical; I think doubt is a good thing. Doubt makes one a critical thinker when necessary. I went through four years of college studying the sciences before going on to graduate school to earn a master's degree in teaching with a license to teach physical sciences, chemistry, earth sciences, and biology. As a result, I eagerly devour reading material that suggests mundane reasons behind psychic phenomena, not because I think I'll hang up my hat and stop doing this work but because I think it will expand our work in both the spiritual and scientific domains.

In short, I want to ask you to try out the techniques in this book not because it would be cool to be the type of person who believes this stuff, but because it works. If it works, you can choose to rationalize an explanation for it. Or you might simply choose to enjoy the mystery and go along for the ride, unconcerned that there is no clear explanation at this point in human history. You might also choose to keep informed about the latest discoveries in neuroscience, physics, and the nature of the mind.

So what if you are just talking to yourself? How is this practice useful? Let's begin looking at this from a psychological viewpoint.

If you've ever had a word on the tip of your tongue, but not been able to recall what you wanted to say, you know that you can't always call to mind everything you have stored in your brain. Even if you know the name of the actress on the screen your friend is asking about, you may not be able to say her name, even though you know it starts with an "S." Later, it may pop into your mind as you are lying in bed, and you'll have to hop out to call your friend. Likewise, you might not be able to remember the tune of a song when somebody asks you under pressure, but during a zoned-out drive in heavy traffic, you'll suddenly be singing it with all the words.

So, how does psychic work tap directly into the subconscious? First, I must point out the obvious dream work as one doorway. Dreams might be one way that we solve life's problems and process learned information acquired during our waking day. However, the surreal nature of a dream is often compounded by its symbolic nature. Reading anything during dreams is difficult because the left half of our brain, the logical portion associated with reading, does not create dreams and therefore cannot operate during them. The right half of the brain, associated with creativity and with the visual imagery seen in dreams, is doing all the work. Thus, these problems being solved by your right brain can only be interpreted once awake. And this interpretation is done by figuring out what those symbols mean.

The good thing about meditation is that you don't have to be asleep to enter the state during which you can retrieve useful information. Your brain activity changes during meditation. Instead of producing the beta waves, as you do when you are alert, your brain makes alpha waves, the same way it does when you begin to doze off. As a result, your perceptions may begin to act in a very interesting way. For example, perfectly sane people can hear voices when their brains are producing alpha waves. So it is natural if you have thought you heard somebody calling your name just as you drift off to sleep or as you shower in the morning while still only half-awake before the day's first cup of coffee.

When you meditate, you not only get the healthful, stress-relieving effects, you can also use it as a form of self-hypnosis to better recall memories of specific events or to make important decisions and solve problems in your life. How do you use your mind as a psychological tool to get answers? Accessing those right-brain visual symbols can be done best through dream work, meditating if you're the sort who receives visual messages, or by scrying forms of divination. Let's take another common example of a woman who isn't sure whether her boyfriend is the man for her.

Josie is in her mid-twenties, and hoped to have the sort of fairy-tale wedding she acted out with her Barbie dolls as a child. Yet, she was rather surprised when Todd, her boyfriend of three years, proposed to her in a steakhouse as they enjoyed a dinner date. In the moment, she instantly said yes, since they had been together for three years. After all, it had been a pretty peaceful relationship. But even as she arrived home to call her parents to tell them the news, she already had doubts. Todd was a good guy and could provide her with a fancy wedding, but he didn't really set off that spark she felt in a previous relationship with her ex-boyfriend, Ryan.

She wondered if she was crazy. Should she nab Todd while he was available, or should she hold out the slim hope that Ryan would come back into her life? Was this doubt a sign that she didn't really love Todd, or was this a natural part of making such a big decision? Perhaps she should just take a giant leap of faith. Josie decided she would tune into her psychic self to answer some of these important questions and make her decision once and for all before going forward.

Josie decided to meditate with some divination in order to ask herself whether she truly loved Todd, and she wanted to go to sleep and dream about what it would be like if they married or if she chose to pursue Ryan; she wanted to see how each scenario might play out in her life. Josie prepared her meditation space with a dark bowl full of water and a lit candle for scrying.

After grounding and centering but before meditation, Josie thought long and hard about Todd and Ryan and asked herself "Who do I love?" She then pushed all thoughts from her mind—even of Todd and Ryan—to quietly meditate in a receptive manner. Feeling relaxed and ready for answers after fifteen minutes, she leaned over the dark bowl filled with water and let her eyes slip into soft focus as she looked through the bowl of water, rather than just at its surface or bottom.

She didn't see anything while water scrying for quite a few minutes, but without being discouraged, she decided to try fire scrying for the answer. She let her eyes go into soft focus again as she looked beyond the flame of the candle rather than *at* it. As the flame danced and leapt, the brighter white parts of the flame and the more yellow parts seemed to take shapes like clouds in the sky. The thin flickering light at the edges of the flame almost looked like dancing spider legs, so she thought to herself what a spider might mean to her.

The first thing that came to mind was how when Todd had seen her jump and scream at a spider in his apartment, he had laughed instead of consoling her or doing something about the creature. His reaction had really hurt her feelings at the time, but she hadn't thought of that event in a couple of years, brushing it off as unimportant. But it must have been important for her to think of it now.

She kept staring at the flame and noticed that its shape looked sort of like an upside-down heart, and the way the wick was jutting into it made it seem like the heart had a long crack. A broken heart that was twisted and upside down? Josie felt she had been "broken" ever since Ryan left her. She never really felt the same for any man since. Josie felt that this visual image truly confirmed that she didn't have deep feelings for Todd. She had just been with him because she felt heartbroken whenever she wasn't with someone.

Josie grounded herself again and extinguished the candle to get ready for bed. She decided she would focus on making herself dream about what she would do with her life if she decided to drop everything with Todd and attempt to rekindle her romance with Ryan. She went to her "memory box" to find some things that reminded her of Ryan. She pulled out a photograph in which the two of them were smiling, but she didn't have any other things to help jar her memory through her other senses, so she studied the picture carefully.

As she stared at the photograph, she willed herself to ask "What would happen if I pursued Ryan?" She turned off the light and settled into bed, drawing out the beginning of the idea in her imagination as sleep took her. She imagined herself looking up his phone number and giving him a call, asking him to spend time with her that weekend. By then, she was already drifting into sleep.

That night, Josie dreamed that she was in Ryan's car with him. He was driving wildly down a winding road. She asked him over and over again to slow down but he would not. Suddenly, headlights lurched out of nowhere from the left-hand side of her field of vision. With the crunch of impact and the sounds of twisting metal, Josie awoke with a start. She switched on a small light by her bed and immediately recorded her dream in the journal she kept there. With a trip to the bathroom and a glass of water to calm her down, she returned to bed and slept peacefully until morning with no more remembered dreams.

The next day, Josie read her dream journal entry from the night before as she ate breakfast. She circled some words that might be symbolic: road, lights, car crash. Next, she thought about what those words might mean about her relationship with Ryan. To her, the winding road seemed to mimic the crazy ups and downs they had. The car crash made her realize how out of control she had felt during that time in her life. Ryan seemed to always have the steering wheel in that relationship, and she was just along for the ride—something she didn't like. She wasn't quite sure at the time what the headlights might mean, but she knew that it might make more sense later when she looked over her dream journal again periodically.

Upon reflection, Josie realized her psychic work revealed that she loved neither Todd nor Ryan. She realized she needed to gain control over her own life before she could have a good partnership with somebody who both created a spark in her heart and was a stable person in her mind. Even though it wasn't the best answer, Josie knew it was the right one. She felt a great peace knowing she finally had the truth. She picked up the phone to call Todd to give him the news that needed to be delivered.

In the above story, you can see how probing the deepest depths of your mind through psychic work may be uncomfortable but very rewarding in the amount of certainty and understanding it gives. Even if you do normally address a deity or a spirit guide when performing psychic readings, I encourage you to work with your own mind as well so you can know yourself more deeply.

As useful a practice as this may be psychologically, some readers may be wondering how to make this form of addressing oneself more spiritual. I have found that you don't have to believe in an external deity to have spirituality. Peeking inside your own subconscious can also be a way to connect with your spiritual side. After all, inscribed over the lintel of the Temple of Apollo, noted for the famous Oracle of Delphi are the words "Know thyself."

Seeking even deeper spiritual wisdom from within can be called consulting your higher self. Your higher self can be a part of you that can be considered a source of spiritual wisdom. In fact, many believe that every person is a god or goddess and that this truth is at the root of the higher self. Some believe that each person's higher self is connected to a universal collective subconscious, and that this instinctive, innate knowledge can be used as a spiritual practice. Similar truths hidden within the higher self may explain how similar deity archetypes have existed independently of one another in different locations around the world.

An example is the Celtic goddess named Brigid, the Catholic Saint Brigid, and a Vodou lwa named Maman Brigit. All three ruled over or helped with similar domains including healing, blacksmithing, and the element of fire. All three are depicted in a remarkably similar way. Even the Vodou lwa is a rare white woman among a collective of mostly dark-skinned entities, since most of the lwa have Afro-Caribbean features. One hypothesis is that this archetype just happened to travel through pantheons, originating in Ireland as Brigid, spreading as Saint Brigid around the world when Christianity rose, and transforming into Maman Brigit when Catholicism and native spirituality collided in Haiti. Another theory is that this personality sprang up independently across time and space from a common need in the collective subconscious of the human race. Regardless of how she came about, something about her was necessary enough for her to either erupt unbidden from multiple cultures, or to endure incredibly across languages, oceans, and thousands of years.

You begin to respect yourself as your own god or goddess when tapping into this instinctual knowledge by working with your higher self. Perhaps you will find new meaning in the commonly used Indian greeting *namaste*, which means "the divinity within me perceives and greets the divinity within you." An intimate and universal connection is thought to be one way people can perform psychic readings for others person using the higher self.

Upon realizing the existence of a higher self, you will find that your psychic potential is limitless. There is a mystic tradition which says that all stored human knowledge can be consulted like a virtual library on the astral plane; the same plane you learned to reach using astral projection and creating your special sacred place during meditation. When you meditate to tap into your higher self, allow yourself to journey to this limitless library. In religious philosophy this library is called the Akashic records; it theoretically holds all the information ever known—past, present, and future. The Akashic records are automatically updated whenever anyone makes a choice that changes his or her future.

The Akashic records can be consulted to perform psychic readings on others through meditation or hypnosis of either yourself or the other person involved so that he or she can read the records. Some people experience the library as actual pages or scrolls that can be read. Many do not, however, which may be due to the limitation of brain anatomy we mentioned earlier that makes it difficult or impossible to read in dreams. As a result, you may find the Akashic records loaded with symbolism you must puzzle out for yourself.

I'll give an example of someone using this method to perform a psychic reading. In this common example, a woman in her mid-forties named Kim confronts the challenge of deciding what to do about her aging mother, Lucy.

Lucy was a spry woman who lived on her own in Arizona, but she was nearing eighty years of age, and both she and Kim worried about the elderly woman's continued ability to be able to care for herself.

Kim offered to let her mother move in with her as is the custom in her culture of origin, but Lucy worried about imposing on her daughter. Kim worried about limiting her mother's lifestyle too soon in her golden years, as well as her ability to cope with her colder Minnesota climate. Lucy, trusting her daughter's choice, asked Kim if she would use her psychic abilities to find out what was the right choice for both of them, for the best and highest good of all.

Going into her quiet meditation space in her bedroom, Kim grounded and centered herself before beginning her psychic work. Since she intended to consult the universal Akashic records about her mother using the power of her higher self, she didn't use a photograph of her mom or any divination tools in her meditation space. However, she did precede meditation with some self-hypnosis. She sat calmly and repeated some suggestions quietly to herself inside her own mind. She told herself: "Through my higher self, I am a Goddess" over and over again for several minutes. Then she repeated the phrase, "I am connected to my mother as I am connected to all people, and I can use my psychic wisdom to help her."

After repeating suggestive phrases like these, she allowed herself to lapse into a quiet meditation for a few more minutes. Then she began to work on visualization. She kept her eyes closed and began to create her sacred space in her mind and thus also on the astral plane. Kim's ideal sacred space was on the shore of a pond filled with water lilies. A stringed instrument played softly, and the smell of a recent rain and fresh flowers filled the air. She stood a moment and allowed the peace of this place to radiate through her.

After spending a bit of time here Kim knew she had to journey to the place where the Akashic records were kept. She told herself that she would find a door to such a place, and she looked around her confidently as she strolled along the edge of her pond. She turned around to see a wooden door jutting straight out of the mossy ground behind her. She approached the door fearlessly, remembering that she controlled this astral place and that nothing could come in or out that she did not allow.

The strength of Kim's visualization was so great that she could feel the cool metal of the doorknob under the palm of her hand and the pressure against her skin as she turned it, pushing the door wide open to view another realm. Though Kim realized that every person might visualize it differently, to Kim the Akashic records looked like a very old library inside somebody's home. All around were comfy but dusty chairs and the smell of old paper and books everywhere in the cozy lines of shelves that seemed to snake out in all directions like a labyrinth.

Kim briefly wondered where she would find the information about her mother but soon realized she would be guided right to it. At ease, she strolled down the first aisle of shelves that caught her eye, running her fingers along the soft old spines of the books. The books had pictures on them rather than titles written in words, so she passed over several books sporting the faces of friends and other loved ones until she landed on the one bearing her mother's smiling image.

As Kim opened the book, she realized that the entire tome was written with pictures rather than words. Some of them seemed to be confusing riddles. She reminded herself that she was looking for the answer about where her mother should live at this stage in her life for the best and highest good of all. She opened the book at random and saw moving pictures on the page as if a television screen was in front of her.

Kim first saw falling snowflakes, which made her think about her worries of her mother not doing well in her cold climate. She waited to see what other images would be associated with that to find the answer to that worry. A light on the page flickered in the corner of her eye. She turned the page and saw what must have been in the distance: a roaring bonfire that looked cheery in wintry weather. When she thought of a cozy fire like that, Kim remembered the wood stove in her childhood home. The hearth fire represented physical heat as well as the love and care of a family to her.

Already Kim felt like she had her answer; she imagined her mother sitting in her own home as she brought her a blanket. She turned the page and a vision appeared right in front of her as her imagination was building it. Since she had built it in the astral plane and it was formed in the Akashic records, Kim knew it was meant to be. She would care for her mother and bring the warmth of greater family love and care into both their lives. She closed the book and carefully put it back on the shelf as if it were a valuable item.

Kim retraced her steps back out the door and into her sacred place. After she opened her eyes from the meditation, she rested a bit and grounded herself fully, feeling giddy from contact with so much information. When she felt relaxed and refreshed, she slowly stood to call her mother and tell her the good news.

In the story above were some pretty specific visualizations, but I want to remind you that yours will most likely be unique. The fact that your imagery may be different doesn't mean it is wrong. Each person perceives things differently according to their life experiences, so if your Akashic records are a computer database and your happy peaceful place is a school jungle gym, great! Don't force yourself to imagine something you think is more "proper." The key is to settle your mind into the emotional state to retrieve information; even if you have to think of some silly things to do so, that's okay.

....

Homework
Solo
Start working with your higher self, as in the examples given in this chapter. You might wish to start out with simple meditation, asking the best part of yourself for answers about an ethical question in your life. Or, you may wish to jump straight into attempting to see the Akashic records through meditation. Working with yourself may mean working with your self-esteem, too, so don't be afraid to

confront self-deprecating thoughts head on. No matter how young you are, or how many mistakes you've made, your higher self is the part of you that is wise.

While exploring yourself, ask yourself frankly about your belief or disbelief in the concept of a deity or deities in the universe. Attempt to define your own beliefs clearly, if only just privately to yourself. If your beliefs seem to be in flux or to change for you often, that is okay. Your belief right now is just a snapshot so that you can develop a prayer before and after readings. Once you have your own idea of god or the gods in your mind, either memorize the prayers provided in this chapter, or develop your own opening and closing prayers or inner monologues that help remind you to be respectful of and grateful for your psychic abilities.

With a Partner

Before I became a professional psychic, I limited myself to reading for friends, family, and members of my spiritual community. As a result, most of the people for whom I performed psychic readings shared my deep beliefs about the gods I addressed during the most spiritual of my readings. When I first branched out to performing psychic readings for the general public, I was terrified that I would run into many people who didn't want me to talk to my gods before, during, or after a psychic reading.

Luckily, I found that most people don't care where I'm getting my information as long as it is right. I want you to push yourself to not be limited to performing psychic readings for people who think just like you too. Choose the mode of psychic reading you are most comfortable with, and offer psychic readings to people who have different belief systems. The person you choose may be a staunch skeptic who thinks you're a kook, or it may be an open-minded Christian, Buddhist, or agnostic who has never had a psychic reading before. If you get turned down, don't worry about it. Just try offering another person the opportunity to have a psychic reading from you.

4 How to Listen

Okay, now you know who you're talking to and you even have the beginnings of a few tools to get their attention and start a conversation. Being a psychic is a little like being in a foreign country full of different customs and an alien language. When I was fifteen, I spent a brief time living with a family in Spain but did not speak the language. At breakfast, they gave me a box of cereal but no milk. I pantomimed the action of drinking a glass of milk and they nodded in response, fetching me a bottle of wine at once. Getting started may be easy for you (or challenging), but things get more difficult the more complex the message you are trying to receive.

Minor confusion and miscommunication is exactly what is happening when you and the source of your psychic information are just getting to know each other and your manners of conversing. When you sit quietly, receptively meditating without allowing your own thoughts to interfere, you've already done the hardest part of listening—being quiet so it may speak to you. But now you have to truly perceive the message before you can understand it and communicate it to others.

Using Forms of Divination to Receive Messages

Divination is whenever a system is used along with a tool or tools to receive psychic messages in an understandable or concrete way. I imagine that the first ancient person to invent a system of divination was tired of waiting around for random psychic flashes to occur during meditation or in everyday life and wanted to create a situation in which random events could be generated, and in addition, outcomes could have an agreed-upon application to questions people wanted answered. Of course, there is no one person who invented divination—it is seen across cultures in many different forms. There are so many different forms that it would be impossible to name them all in this book.

The most popular forms in American culture seem to change. I remember when I was practicing professionally at the end of the 1990s tarot cards were all the rage. The popularity of the tarot as a tool was mostly due to pop culture commercial spokespersons depicted using the tarot. Consisting of seventy-eight cards, the tarot card deck is used to tell fortunes. Psychic hotlines were experiencing their heyday. Now, however, although the hotlines still exist, many psychic readers advertise that they do not use tarot cards or any tools in their working.

Professional psychics eschewing the use of cards is not a reflection of the value of divination tools such as tarot cards; rather, it mirrors the shift in public perception and its ever-changing views of what a psychic truly is or does. There are those who believe someone is somehow less of a psychic if a deck of cards or any other tool must be consulted. I personally do not feel that this is the case though I choose whether or not to use tools depending on the situation, client, and question at hand. I believe that tools are an aid that can produce amazing and wonderful results, and if clients are going to nitpick how you solve their problems and empower them, then perhaps they aren't the sort of people who need your help anyway.

Even if you have been successful thus far with learning how to be a psychic without using any divination tools whatsoever, I highly recommend choosing one in order to compare and contrast experiences with tools and without. I often use the analogy that just as a hammer and saw are both used on wood, you might choose one or the other (or neither) depending on what it is you need to do. In the case of psychic work we must consider the person doing the asking in addition to the question itself.

Symbolism

Chances are no matter what perception you seem to be using to acquire your information, it is coming to you in the form of symbols rather than literal quotes. The good news is that you don't have to fear if you see something rather disturbing, such as fire or death. The bad news is that the real work is ahead of you, in solving the riddles your own brain deals to you in order to transfer messages from your subconscious right-brain to your conscious mind.

A symbol is something that stands for something else. So while a fire might seem like a frightening thing to actually *happen*, it represents warmth, the home's hearth, or transformation, since it changes what it touches into ash. Figuring out your symbols is like learning a new language and can take a lifetime of study. Don't feel discouraged if you tend to get confused when a new symbol turns up in your perceptions. Make a guess and see if it applies in the context. Interpreting symbols will take some trial and error, so make sure to record in a journal, like you hopefully already do when symbols appear in your dreams.

There are two major methods for dealing with and interpreting symbolic psychic messages, so I will introduce you to each and discuss the pros and cons. Afterwards, you may decide which is best for you. Understand that your method may change during your life as a psychic or even from reading to reading, and that is okay. As always, keep a record in your journal to see if your accuracy improves over time depending on the techniques you try.

The first way of dealing with symbols is to decide their meaning before you see them and then look for them. The benefit of this method is that there are already numerous, huge bodies of literature that describe what symbols might mean in different cultures or across cultures. The method of using predetermined symbols also lets you interpret readings right away rather than spending a lot of time figuring out the riddles your brain has set in front of you. To get started with this method, you might wish to begin looking in dream dictionaries and books on scrying divination forms to see the definitions others have found for various symbols. Then, each time you dream, meditate, or scry you can immediately record the symbols you perceive and consult your references for an instant interpretation.

The first problem with this method is that your associations with many symbols may differ greatly from those of others. The example I often give is that bats are my favorite animals, but they strike fear in the hearts of many. So, while seeing a bat would be a good sign for me, it might be a symbol of fear or death for another person who associates bats with Halloween, skeletons, etc. Likewise, a slab of meat might mean sustenance and delicious dining to many people, but as a vegetarian, I would see it as distasteful and representing death.

You can get around this problem by thinking up and agreeing on specific symbols. If you choose to work with spirit guides, you can call a meeting with them during a meditation and agree on specific things. For example:

"Whenever the answer is yes, I want you to show me a happy face. Whenever love is the subject, I want you to show me a heart." Asking for specific symbols gets around the problem of seeing symbols that don't make sense to you. That being said, one problem that remains with this method is that you can tend to bias yourself towards seeing what you want to see or hearing what you want to hear. If you look hard enough for a happy face or a heart, you will most likely find a way to see one no matter the real answer.

As a result, this method is particularly susceptible to your own personal bias if you are already looking for specific symbols. The only way to minimize this bias is to allow yourself to learn your own symbolism, which is far more vast than all the dream dictionaries in the world. The benefit of this method is that you will not be limited to a small vocabulary of potential messages. Unfortunately, this method takes longer to learn and can sometimes leave you still confused after a thorough study of a particularly mysterious message.

The other issue with the second method—and it is debatable whether or not this is a problem—is that your meanings for your own symbols may shift and change over time as you experience more and more things in life. I personally think that this process is natural, and will add strength and depth to your psychic readings over time. But it must be said that some psychics believe that allowing symbols to change their meaning does nothing but cause confusion and make readings less accurate.

I greatly prefer this latter method, however, because I believe that the mental challenge of figuring out these psychic messages is part of the process. Over time I think it has allowed me to become a better and more versatile reader, and I am more able to quickly pick up new psychic reading techniques. Seeing images doesn't have to be a hard and fast language, like how letters represent specific sounds and words when arranged in specific patterns. Instead, the symbols should act as prompts, sending your mind to a specific train of thought.

For example, just this past Halloween, I performed a crystal ball reading to speak with my deceased father. The communication was during a time of divination set within a ritual celebration of the holiday. Among other symbols that revealed themselves to me, I saw that the occlusions in the crystal seemed to be shaped like a bow and arrow. Now, taken as a specific symbol, this might be associated with hunting or with going for your goals. But I used the context of my conversation with my father and my memories of discussions with my parents in order to draw a different meaning.

I had been consulting the crystal ball in order to talk with my late father about my newborn daughter, who was just one month old at the time. When I saw the bow and arrow, I remembered a discussion I had with my parents when my father was alive. He and my mother always seemed to give advice together as a unit. He was talking about how difficult it was trying to help me avoid mistakes that he had made when he was a child, and I was frustrated as a teenager because I naturally thought I was smarter than he was. I now know that wasn't true, although I may have had a better head on my shoulders as a teenager than he had in his teens. During the course of this conversation, my mother told me that raising a child was like shooting an arrow. You could hold the bow, aim, and pull back the string as far as you liked, but once it was released you had to just let it fly where it may.

The entire memory flooded back to me in an instant after seeing little flecks of light that seemed to be a bow and arrow. Understanding the meaning through memory was a much richer interpretation for me than if I had just opened a book and looked up what "arrow" meant, and it gave me a deeper emotional reaction of peace and confidence and perhaps just a little bit of fatalism with regards to my queries about parenting.

Luckily for me, I made that connection in the moment, but a new psychic can find it hard to relax the mind enough to allow it to make those associations. If I had drawn a blank upon seeing the symbol, I would have simply written it down and gone back to it later for further analysis. Have you ever been in the middle of a sentence and had a word be right on the tip of your tongue, and yet not remember what you wanted to say? Sometimes the word will suddenly come to you later during the day when you're not pressuring your brain to produce it on the spot. Have faith that this same phenomenon will happen with symbols as well.

If you find this process cumbersome, have faith too that it will become increasingly smooth and quicker with experience. The sooner you start trying and the more frequently you work on your psychic symbolism, the sooner you will find yourself fluent with the symbolic language of your own subconscious. Even though it may be frustrating for a beginner, I suggest that you devote the time to study your own internal language of symbols, and slowly build your own dictionary of meanings in your journal.

Coincidences

Since many psychic flashes of understanding can be confused with chance events that seem more meaningless, let's talk about coincidences. On one side of the spectrum, you have those who think that everything unusual is most likely just a coincidence, and on the other side there are those who think that there is a reason behind everything. I must admit that I fall on the latter side of the spectrum, though I have followed my intuition to both pots of gold and wild goose chases at different times in my life. However, the presence of coincidences is not a factor so confounding that you should throw up your hands and stop trying to differentiate altogether. In fact, considering coincidences is a big part of any investigation and experiment.

Since coincidences can be confusing, a journal logging your psychic flashes or predictions is key. Then, thinking a little bit about basic probability can help you decide which experiences of yours deserve further effort to develop and which might be nothing more than coincidences, mistakes, or things that are too unreliable at present to be worth your time. Note that uncertainty is not necessarily a reason to throw out everything.

A couple of years ago I was working with a forensic researcher who was interested in collecting data about using psychics to solve crimes. When I asked him how he would deal with the uncertainty that is natural from human error, he pointed out that police dogs, which are commonly used to solve crimes, are extremely fallible. Yet their results are still used as evidence admissible in court. He drew to my attention the FBI's use of dogs that incorrectly identified Steven Hatfil as a suspect in the 2001 anthrax attacks. The existence of false leads doesn't mean that your psychic powers are worthless, just that critical thinking is required.

For those of you who might have a phobia of mathematics, I won't get into deep statistical analysis here, but I do wish to draw your attention to the use of quantitative data as a tool. In just a moment I'll more fully explain Zener cards, tools used to test for ESP. For now, all you need to know is that each card has one of five symbols. Thus, each time you draw a card, you should only guess correctly by coincidence one-fifth of the time, or twenty percent. If you were trying to psychically know the result of a coin toss, there are only two options, heads or tails. You can only guess correctly by coincidence about one out of every two tosses, or fifty percent of the time.

Keep your mind alert for ways to start looking at the numbers associated with your psychic flashes, even if you don't work too deeply on analysis. If you find yourself wondering whether it is a coincidence that you look over at your sister's photograph a few seconds before she calls you on the telephone and it seems to happen every time, don't be afraid to start collecting some data in your journal. In this case, you'd simply have to start noting how often you glance at your sister's photograph, perhaps by putting a little checkmark on a piece of paper by your seat. You might find that you actually stare at it often when you're thinking without even noticing it. If that page fills up with checkmarks, you might be barking up the wrong tree. But if your eyes rest on that corner of the room quite rarely, you may have something to investigate further.

Continuously finding that the things you'd hoped were psychic phenomena aren't consistently reproducible may feel like a frustrating exercise. Remember that this doesn't mean your ideas about their importance were wrong. There may still be something to even the most unlikely and unrepeatable of experiences. However, if you want to be a psychic, it does you no good to spread yourself too thin and doggedly keep trying work that is not your best. Instead, use these observations to find out what your focus should be. Work on those things at which you seem to naturally excel, and come back later to revisit those things that seemed to just be coincidences but for which you still hold out hope. As you develop some aspects of your psychic abilities, you may find that other areas of your work will improve. You may also be able to later gain measurable results much more quickly.

Exercise To Test Your ESP

Zener cards can be used with a partner to see if guessing is a coincidence or real ESP. These cards have images on them such as a star or a set of wavy lines. They were developed by psychologist Karl Zener in order to conduct experiments with clairvoyance, the ability to have true visions of what one is not physically seeing. If no psychic ability is assumed, a person should guess the right card one out of five times, since there are a total of five possible images on the cards. Perhaps for the same reason that the concern of a mother for her child can encourage natural telepathy, I find that telepathic success is easier to accomplish with somebody when he or she has an emotional connection with the thought message being passed along, and it is hard to get that excited about a set of squiggly lines or a square. So, grab a willing partner and make some alternative card sets of your own with some index cards or pieces of paper.

Start out by making a collaborative card set that depicts things that evoke similar emotions for each of you. There will be a card each for happiness, sadness, anger, love, and fear. For each card, decide together what evokes that same emotion for both of you. For example, perhaps both of you have a phobia of spiders, maybe kittens make you both happy, and there might be a scene in a specific movie that can always make the two of you cry. For each emotion, draw a depiction of that thing or event that both of you share on the card to jog your memory and your emotions.

As for working with the cards and each other, I highly recommend starting out by trying to figure out which card your partner is thinking about without looking at your partner. Not seeing your partner is important because the emotion might show on your partner's face or in his or her body language, even if your partner insists that they have a very good poker face. Many people have a flash of emotion called a micro-expression that can't be suppressed when first beginning to experience an emotion, even if it is rapidly covered up. You want your work to be the result of your psychic ability rather than your powers of observation.

Have your partner draw a card, and then stare at and think strongly about the card and attempt to experience the emotion the card evokes. You can try sitting back to back with your partner, or even holding hands. Some people find that a physical connection seems to aid their psychic connection. Eventually, you might wish to try practicing while in the other room, or even on a telephone at a greater distance.

After you've mastered this telepathy technique using your set of cards with shared emotional cues, each of you can make an individual set without showing each other the cards. On your second set of cards, the emotional cues should be unique to you, so don't discuss them as you are making them. Each of you should make a set for the same group of emotions as before. This time, however, feel free to think openly about whatever evokes that emotion the strongest. So, while your friend might draw his spouse on the "love" card, you might draw chocolate, and that's okay!

Now, I asked you not to show each other what you had on your cards, and that's just to have a little fun to see if you can try the same experiment and actually "see" what is on the cards. Of course, this experiment only works out once per card set, because after that you'll know what your partner associates with each emotions for this particular card set. However, it can be fun to see whether your telepathy has developed to the level of being able to make this leap. Don't be discouraged if you only get the emotion and not the picture. Often the emotions are the first to cross that person-to-person barrier with telepathy, and the other imagery may soon follow.

Omens

Monday's child is fair of face,
Tuesday's child is full of grace,
Wednesday's child is full of woe,
Thursday's child has far to go,
Friday's child is loving and giving,
Saturday's child works hard for a living,
But the child who is born on the Sabbath Day
Is bonny and blithe and good and gay.

The above is a popular fortune-telling nursery rhyme that illustrates specific omens. But that's not the only psychic trick that you might have learned as a child. A black cat crossing your path, a spilled shaker of salt, or a dropped mirror that shatters into many pieces might all make some people wonder if they're in for bad luck. A broom falling over from its place in the corner might mean that company will soon be coming. And then there's all that weather lore: "Red sky at night, sailor's delight. Red sky at morning, sailors take warning." Before my parents won a small lottery that afforded our family the opportunity for travel, they saw a double rainbow they took as a portent of good fortune that urged them to buy a lottery ticket. The aforementioned occurrences are all omens that indicated either good or bad luck and might cause one to choose to take or avoid a particular action.

Omens and divination are slightly different things. Both have to do with using things around you in order to make predictions or to do other psychic work, but while divination involves using specialized tools and a system for the task, omens are accidental events or situations that have meaning. Omens are fun to share and are countless in number. You could spend the rest of your life collecting small bits of lore, but one of the tricky problems with omens is that they often mean different things depending on the culture of origin. For example, seeing a bat is a positive Chinese omen for luck, but a negative European one meaning death. Whether the number thirteen is good or bad luck is a similar dichotomy.

The other problem with omens is that because they are random events, you can't use most of them as a reliable source of information on a regular basis. For example, unless you own a black cat, one is unlikely to be around to either cross your path or not if you're checking to see if today is a lucky day to buy a house. However, other omens are fairly frequent to the point where they are a bit systematic, almost like divination. For example, fortune-telling using birds can be used in areas where birds are usually located. A bird flying to the right can mean good luck, while one flying to the left is bad news. The exception to this case are owls, where the rule is reversed.

A gray area in which omens and divination begin to meet and mix a bit is with numerology. Numerology can be applied to names and dates of birth in many ways to generate meanings about a person's character and destiny. However, extra meanings associated with numbers can enrich your interpretation of omens. So, while two birds flying to the right might give emphasis to your hopes for luck in love, eight birds flying to the right might give more attention to luck in your school-to-work transition. As mentioned with regard to the number thirteen, the meanings of numbers vary widely, but here are some examples to help you start thinking about the numbers that show up in your life in the form of omens.

1. Leadership, aggression, striking out on a new path

2. Love, meeting someone or something new, striking a balance

3. New creative pursuits, sharing, communication

4. Stability, the beginning of a foundation, the home

5. Shifting change, restlessness, chaos

6. Learning and growth, leadership

7. What others think about you, hidden knowledge

8. Growing to a higher potential, rewards for hard work

9. Happiness, luck, potential

How Do I Know I'm Not Crazy?

A client of mine was watching television one night, not thinking about anything in particular, when she suddenly saw something big and white from the corner of her eye. Frightened, she didn't turn her head towards it, afraid of what she might see. She turned off the television and went straight to bed. Knowing that I was writing this book, she asked me to include a section on what to expect as your psychic powers develop. After all, to some this practice may seem like you're just talking to yourself and then becoming overly excited about coincidences. On the other hand, it might look like magical thinking is sending you on a dangerous downward spiral into a mental breakdown. Think about both of these possibilities frankly so you can watch for signs that you're either wasting your time or driving yourself nuts.

What if you have no doubt of your psychic abilities and that frightens you every once in a while? What if, like the client mentioned earlier, it is the certainty that frightens you? Where is the line drawn between psychic and just plain crazy? Stories are passed around by practitioners of magic and the occult regarding how misuse can cause madness—can the same thing be caused by psychic work? Or worse yet, is being a psychic conditional upon being insane? Are psychic experiences just a symptom of a disease?

I admit this subject is one close to my heart due to my own personal issues. Like one in four American adults, I have a mental illness. I had to ask myself some hard questions and I still do fairly regularly to keep some perspective on the issue for the sake of my clients and to manage my own health. In my case, my mental illness developed suddenly, years after I had already become a professional psychic and after a lifetime of practicing psychic work on a personal level. My mother, who also has worked as a professional psychic, remains untouched by mental disorder of any kind, however.

I do not believe that psychic work caused my own mental illness. However, I share this with you because when I point out when it is time to get professional help, I want my readers to know that I've been there. When I give such advice it is only out of compassion and because there may be genuine cause for concern. I am not being dismissive because I don't think the presence of mental illness means one should swear off psychic work. I'm living proof that both conditions can coexist, and I became a certified counselor in my state so I could advise those who are well and be connected with referrals in my community when somebody seems to need mental help.

The tricky part is that some things sensitive psychics experience can mimic serious mental illnesses, and these experiences might increase if you are working actively to increase your psychic sensitivity. For example, a very good friend in my spiritual worship group noticed that her psychic abilities began increasing rapidly as soon as she began working sincerely on her spirituality with us. Her clairvoyant and clairaudient psychic abilities took the form of some rather frightening experiences, including seeing things and hearing things that kept her awake at night and made her feel like she was going crazy.

Since seeing and hearing things are some of the symptoms of serious psychosis, how can you know whether you are becoming more psychic or succumbing to schizophreniform disorder—or both? Since I have experienced both, I often have clients and friends come to me when they have perfectly normal experiences that frighten them in this way. I can certainly give you some answers as to how to tell the difference.

The first and most important clue is the amount of disturbance your experiences create in your life. If you have a moment every now and again that causes you to wonder whether the experience was valid or not and then turn off the television and go to sleep, then these are normal moments as a human being. However, if you find your ability to work, sleep, eat, or leave the house is affected by your fears or your experiences, something is going wrong regardless of whether what you are perceiving is real or not. At that point you need to seek some outside help.

Likewise, feelings of anxiety that are so great you think you are becoming suicidal should *never* be ignored. Even though working with the dead can be an emotionally upsetting part of psychic readings, if you feel like you might harm yourself or others, get help right away. From my experiences with mental illness, I have an important caveat for those who seem to have psychic experiences that come in the form of seeing things and hearing things, as well as other senses. While in ancient times such people may have been revered as shamans, in these modern times if somebody hears voices or sees things, these visions are considered to be hallucinations. Earlier, I pointed out that hearing voices when in an alpha brain wave state, such as when you are just falling asleep or just waking up is normal. Another thing that is normal is "hearing" a voice in your imagination in the same way that you might hear your own voice telling you not to forget to put gas in the car on your way to work. Even if it is another voice that is not yours, if you seem to hear it with your mind and not your ears, this is normal. The same goes for "seeing" visions with your mind's eye.

However, if you hear things that aren't there and they seem to come to you through your ears like real sounds, then you have something you need to investigate. The same applies if you see visions that seem to be perceived with your physical eyes the same way you see everything else. Experiences with hearing or seeing things don't automatically mean you're crazy, but they do need to be looked into to make sure that you don't have a problem even if you aren't bothered by hearing or seeing such things.

You should not ignore the potential for problems because in addition to being potentially caused by psychic ability or mental illness, hallucinations can also be caused by life-threatening conditions such as brain tumors, seizure disorders, or organ failure. You must get those things ruled out by visiting a compassionate general physician and following up with any referrals necessary. Remember, these are all things I went through as well, even getting an MRI and a CAT scan, so I can say firsthand that you shouldn't let anxiety about the process prevent you from getting checked out. After you come through with a clean bill of health, possibly after your first visit to a doctor or after you manage any existing illnesses, you can relax and explore your psychic ability without worries in the back of your mind getting in the way.

....

Homework

Solo

Begin a symbol dictionary in your psychic journal, and choose a form of divination to study at your own pace. If the system you choose bores you, go ahead and choose another. There's no reason to stick with one system if it means banging your head against the wall, getting no answers. Divination isn't about torturing yourself with a random discipline—find a tool that is easy for you.

Since fluency with any form of divination requires diligent practice, I suggest that if you do find a form of divination you enjoy, begin doing a daily reading for yourself and recording the results in your journal. For example, if you choose tarot cards, pick a "card of the day" that represents the day ahead of you each morning.

With a Partner

Test whether or not you have ESP by using the exercise in this chapter with a partner. Don't be too discouraged if you feel like you failed the test. Though Zener cards were designed to test ESP, I think they test clairvoyance more than anything else. You may not be the visual clairvoyant type.

Your psychic ability may be more in tune with your other senses and that's okay.

All these homework assignments are designed for you to jump in and try things out with the idea that you can work more with the things that seem to come more naturally at first. No psychic comes equipped with the same talents in the beginning. Developing your existing talents and discovering new skills take time. Put your set of cards away and study another form of psychic work for a while. You can come back to your cards later to see if your skills have improved.

5 Communicating Psychically

As might be expected, communicating psychically isn't always the same as holding an ordinary conversation with another person. Sometimes it may be strikingly similar if you hold a chat with a spirit or a deity over tea during a visualization, or if you are the sort of clairvoyant who can see ghosts in the same room as clearly as if they were another living person. Other times, communicating psychically is like receiving strange riddles in the form of pictures or hearing a foreign voice over a crackly telephone line.

This chapter introduces another form of psychic communication called channeling. Here, the psychic acts like the telephone itself and the message comes directly from the spirit to other people through the psychic. Acting as a conduit for a message from a spirit doesn't have to feel as scary as being completely possessed. Taking in and passing on the spirit's message can feel as easy and natural as breathing; you can take in a spirit's energies and messages gently and then release them to those around you with care.

Spirits

The chapter ahead will help you get acquainted with the different types of spirits with whom you can communicate psychically. You can be the conduit through which the spirits of the dead can speak to the living so deceased loved ones can pass messages on to the bereaved. However, you can also communicate psychically with dead people who never knew the people with whom they are now conversing. Yes, this can mean the spirits of celebrities, as is most often claimed by sensationalist people immediately following the death of one, however the most useful common application may be to channel spirit guides.

Spirit guides are helper entities many believe made an agreement before each of us were born to help us throughout our life challenges, offering advice, and even a helping or healing hand. Spirit guides may once have been living people, and indeed many psychic mediums profess to have spirit guides of fantastic origins. For example, medium Rose Vanden Eynden believes she has a healing spirit guide who was once a Native American brave. Eynden teaches that every person has a team of spirit guides ready to assist when summoned. Spirit guides include a master guide as a great teacher, joy guide, protector guide, doctor teacher who acts like a professor, and a doctor chemist who can act as a healer, in addition to many more potential guides.

Getting in touch with your spirit guides may be the start of a very fulfilling, lifelong relationship with entities who can provide you with a steady stream of accurate psychic information. You can also connect with the guides of others. I have a client who regularly comes to me to ask for a message from her guide. So even if you choose not to work with your own guides directly, it might be helpful to consider whether you are willing and able to connect with the spirit guides of others.

How does one go about connecting with spirit guides? Spiritualist mediums like Eynden suggest using the tool of meditation you have already established. Before your meditation session, you can request one guide (your protector guide, for example) to make his or her presence known to you. Upon meditation, you can then be receptive to any visions, sounds, or other perceptions your guide gives to you. Be patient with yourself as you develop this capability, as it may take several meditation sessions to obtain a result that feels satisfying to you.

How to Connect with Spirit Guides

1. During meditation, ask for a spirit guide who wants to help you as your primary intermediary to make himself or herself known to you. Introduce yourself. Attempt to learn this spirit guide's name,

appearance, and other identifying features; such as where he or she likes to stand near you.

2. During subsequent meditations, decide on a system of communication based on what psychic skills work best for you. For example, if you are clairvoyant, you might tell your spirit guide that when an answer is "yes," you want him or her to show you a green check mark.

3. When you have a question, ask for your spirit guide to help you and to make the best answer known to you.

When attempting to contact a dead person you knew during life, it has been mentioned already that you can ask for that person to appear in your dreams for you. You may also wish to request that he or she meet you during a meditation session. If you have been asked to contact the deceased on behalf of somebody else, solo meditation and dream work are not the only tools at your disposal. Use any tools of divination you wish in order to make the experience more valuable to the bereaved. After all, it may feel more rewarding to him or her to watch you turn over a tarot card that he or she can see, rather than just listening to you rattle off messages. Images shown on divination tools such as tarot cards can have special meaning to the bereaved, and can take you out of the channeling role to help you connect the two more directly through the tools at your disposal.

How to Speak with the Spirits of the Dead

1. Ask out loud for a deceased relative you know to appear for you in your dreams.

2. Whether or not the first step worked, try meditating and asking a deceased relative you know to accompany you.

3. Whether or not the first two steps worked, use a divination method of your choice and ask aloud for a deceased relative you know to answer questions for you.

4. Go back to the first three steps until you can do them all. When you are comfortable with each of the first three steps, you can try a mediumship session with other bereaved people present or to call on a deceased person you do not know.

Séances

Up until now, I've discussed how you can communicate directly with spirits as a psychic to get messages for yourself. Psychic communication can also be done for others with the psychic acting as the middleman in the presence of the bereaved during a mediumship session known as a séance. Traditionally, a séance is performed in a group setting, seated around a table. A mediumship session may be an exciting prospect if you have seen séances in movies in which the spirits rapped on the walls or levitated the table while the shocked guests held hands by spooky candlelight. In the heyday of mediumship, these activities did take place, though later the levitating table and knocking sounds were often exposed as parlor tricks by charlatans.

Though it would be exciting to conjure flying furniture and ectoplasm to take the form of spirit people, you will have to settle for the usual séance being far less fantastical if you want to be a psychic. Make sure the bereaved is also content with a mellow séance before enlisting your help.

When mediumship was used as entertainment, the number of people involved was important, and the number five was often avoided due to its connection with the occult. However, any small group can hold a séance, though I suggest you keep the number small as possible to avoid distraction. Only allow people who will be respectful and sincere, lest it affect the willingness of the deceased to participate.

Though several deceased persons can be contacted during a single séance, I suggest concentrating on only one deceased person per séance session if you are a beginner so you don't confuse and mix up the messages as they come through. Learning the skills of contacting the dead is one thing, and another skill must be learned on top of that to get them to line up one by one and take turns speaking. Attempting to learn both skills at once might be less than successful.

A real séance can be performed either standing or seated, however I do recommend a table. A table can be used to hold the divination tools if you wish to use them. You may wish to place a scrying mirror, crystal ball, or bowl filled with water or milk in the center in order to attempt to see visions within them. The table can also be used to create an ancestor altar as a shrine to honor the deceased to give love and respect in trade for the contact made.

If several bereaved persons are in attendance, you may wish to request that each bring something that reminds them of the deceased before coming to the séance. Possible mementos might be a photograph, a treasured item such as a piece of jewelry, or even a meal or food item the deceased used to love. If a photograph is used, make sure no people who are still living are included in the picture.

After the table and chairs have been arranged and the objects placed on the table, you may begin the séance with prayer if you are a believer in deities, or with a ritual if desired. Some believe that a protective circle should be formed about the table in order to hold in the spirits or energies called within, or keep out spirits or entities you don't wish to have present. If you have your own spiritual tradition that includes casting circles, feel free to use your own. I will include a generic sample ritual opener here.

Begin with the attendees already seated and the table prepared. Before all else, you must ground yourself. Situations in which you must ground quickly are where your practice comes in handy since if you are not completely at ease with grounding, you may find it difficult to do so on the spot—especially in the face of an exciting event such as your first séance, surrounded by people watching your every move.

You may wish to start by sweeping the floor slowly with a broom, focusing your intent on clearing the space in order to welcome in your intended spirit. Walk in a circle, sweeping the area counterclockwise three times, beginning closer to the center, and ending with the last circle at the edges of the room or designated space. Sweep the last of the literal or imaginary debris out the door and lay the broom down across the entryway.

At this point, you can draw the circle, delineating the ritual space. Creating a circle can be done with an imaginary line traced with your finger and imagined in your mind's eye, or it can be a literal line made with a length of rope, chalk, salt, or flour. The literal circle may be recommended for a group setting with inexperienced participants so everyone can see the ritual space you are envisioning.

Now that you have cleared out and set up the space, it is time to begin inviting some positive energies and entities to help you. You can start by making your circle into a microcosm (a smaller representation of the universe at large) by welcoming in the energies of each of the four directions—these correspond to the elements. You may wish to have a candle posted at each direction and perhaps a small representation of each element. For example, at the east you might have some incense representing the element of air. At the south you can have a lantern to represent fire, at the west a bowl of water, and at the north a potted plant or a bowl of salt to represent earth.

Go around to each of the four quarters in turn to light the candles, starting in the east. You will greet each direction in turn, and with it all of the symbolism of that direction. Combined, they represent everything in the universe, so you call all of those positive things and energies to your aid. Now that your circle is complete, you can call the entities to its center. If you wish, begin by addressing any deities you would like to be present to guide you as you work with the deceased.

Before summoning the dead, it is appropriate to join hands around the table with all the guests present, which is one thing you may have seen in popular media about séances that *does* happen to be a real technique. You may wish to hold hands with everyone's thumbs pointing left, so that each person has one hand under and one hand over the hand of the person next to him or her. Pointing the thumbs left is so that the energy flows in one direction, specifically clockwise. A directional configuration is helpful if you need to increase the energy in your circle, in particular when you perceive that "nothing is happening."

If however the opposite is true and you find yourself easily overwhelmed by energy or "too much happening," it may be better to have everyone in the circle place their hands palms down on the table with fingers spread and move their hands closer to the center of the circle until each person's pinkie finger is touching the smallest fingers of the people on either side to complete the circuit. Touching hands without grasping is useful so that if any one person becomes overwhelmed, he or she can withdraw his or her hands quickly without being a distraction or feeling embarrassed.

Next you may request the presence of the deceased, perhaps allowing the bereaved to ask for him or her to come to speak with them. Explain why you as a group wish to talk to him or her, whether it be simply to express love or for a more pressing matter like finding a missing will.

At this stage in the movies, you would ask the deceased to make his or her presence known, and a knocking would be heard or the candles would flicker. This is not necessary, however. Check to make sure you are still feeling grounded and begin your meditation. It is vital to have previously practiced meditation until you are completely able and comfortable doing so under "performance pressure."

Allow yourself plenty of time to sit in silent meditation, even if you have divination tools in front of you. You may turn to them later. Warn your guests that you will be doing this, if you feel self-conscious. The error beginners make here is in cutting the time too short, rather than waiting too long to receive messages. A minute can feel like an eternity when you feel anxious for a response or pressured to perform, but chances are that little time has passed even if you are starting to feel impatient.

After your quiet meditation, you can take time to communicate with the bereaved any perceptions that you may have had during the experience. They might wish to ask questions for clarification, but they may not. One person can be designated as a scribe if desired so that the words you speak can be recorded. I know that when I am channeling or in a deep trance state, I often cannot remember what I said immediately afterward, similar to the forgetfulness common with dreaming.

Losing a memory of a dream or meditation may be due to the brain entering the alpha wave state associated with early sleep, or it may be due to the more spiritual challenge of bringing the information from one world into another. After all, you are performing as a Shaman in this state and retracing the ancient path of the Hero's Journey told in many stories across time and culture. Just as Cinderella's coach turned back into a pumpkin at midnight after the ball, you may find that your memory of what went on during the séance fades or changes.

If you have divination tools present, it is appropriate to use them to address the specific questions to the deceased from the bereaved or to find out if there are any more things the deceased wishes to say. Allow the bereaved time to speak aloud to the deceased or to vent their emotions.

After the work is done, it is time to close the circle in the same manner it was created. Begin by thanking the deceased for attending and bidding them to depart in peace. If this step is skipped, the deceased may think that it is okay to stick around, which might be disturbing to anyone who lives or occupies that space now or in the future. Even if it is your own home and you feel completely comfortable with ghosts, it is best to allow the spirit to leave freely out of respect. Besides, you won't be the only person to ever own your property.

Make sure you thank and allow each of the four quarters' energies you called into your circle to dissipate harmlessly. I've heard many stories of forgotten elements or haphazard circle closings gone awry, such as one friend who had leaky pipes in his home after forgetting to thank and dismiss water in the west and another friend who had several kitchen fires before making sure to properly acknowledge the fire energies in the south.

Remember to thank your deities if you chose to invite their guidance during your work, by closing with a prayer. Next, walk around counter-clockwise to dismiss the four quarters, extinguishing each candle in turn, beginning in the northern direction.

You don't need to sweep your circle again, unless you feel it completes the ritual, but you do need to take down the external circle that you drew. You can do so by cleaning up the outline that you made, or by walking around and visualizing drawing the energy back up into your hand and grounding it into the earth. Some choose to visualize breaking open the circle at a single point by cutting an imaginary hole. My teacher visualizes it collapsing like a tent after the supporting poles have been removed. Sometimes I imagine the circle as a sphere made of rotating hoops on each axis, and these hoops can unite with each other and then withdraw from whence they came.

I'll give an example of a mediumship session so you can see the order of events and how one might choose to use the mental tools I've given to connect with those who have died and crossed over to the other side. In this example, the psychic asks a deceased family member for help. Anyone can ask their ancestors for aid. Deceased family members will help as often as they wish, which for some personalities might mean daily assistance; others might show up only for special occasions. Experiment until you find the ancestors who most often want to work effectively with you or with those you help, as in the story below.

A psychic medium named Chloe had a best friend named Richard, who had recently suffered the loss of his father in an automobile accident. Luckily, Richard knew that his father, Daniel, had written a will; his siblings were the type to fight bitterly over their father's treasured possessions, as they had already lost their mother to breast cancer several years prior. Unfortunately, the location of the will remained unknown—Daniel didn't expect that he would die anytime soon.

Chloe invited Richard as well as his two sisters, Maggie and Rachel, over to her home for the mediumship sitting. She then set the stage. She cleaned up her dining room and arranged four chairs around the table. She put candles about, gathered up all the divination tools she had in the house, and set them in the middle of the table. Her tools included a deck of playing cards, a pendulum, a lit candle, and bowl of milk for scrying. She added a pen and notebook to the table so they could record what happened during the sitting.

When her guests arrived, she showed them to their seats and started a brief discussion about what was going to happen to make sure she had their informed consent. They sat together uneasily, shooting daggers at each other with their eyes. Their grief had made them combative and they couldn't agree on how to split Daniel's belongings. She explained to them that she was going to try to directly contact their deceased father and asked if that was all right with them. Chloe pointed out that since this was real, there was the potential that their father might have unpleasant things to say to them if he wished. She asked if everyone was emotionally prepared for such a message. She showed them her divination tools, describing each and how it was used. She asked them if they were comfortable with her using them during the sitting if she wished. After each person had agreed to the terms of the sitting, she prepared to begin the work, explaining what she was doing as she did it.

Next, Chloe asked each person present individually if there were any questions they wished to ask their father. Because the grief was still very fresh, no one had immediate questions that jumped to mind; they simply hoped they would be able to connect with their daddy once more. Each agreed that finding the will was the most important message that could be imparted at this time so they could have some closure to the squabble and move forward with healing the family. Chloe asked if anyone was willing to be a scribe so the messages could be recorded for later review and analysis. Maggie agreed to the task, taking the pen and notebook to her place at the table.

After sweeping the circle area, Chloe had everyone join hands before she grounded and centered herself, explaining that if they gave their permission, she would be the conduit through which they could ground their excess energy as well. She gave them all a bit of extra time during this step so that she could allow herself to feel the energy from everyone flowing through her and harmlessly into the earth. Chloe set up the circle, said a prayer (she believed in a deity), and asked for help receiving the right and true answers for her guests that night. Finally, she invited Daniel to come into their circle and give a message to his children about where the will might be located. Then she lapsed into silent, receptive meditation to wait for a response, if any.

Chloe did not force any expectations, nor visualizations at this time. After a while she began to feel very funny. As she slid peacefully into a trance, she felt so relaxed that it seemed like she was in another place even though she knew she hadn't left the room. The temperature felt a little cooler, and she seemed to feel the presence of somebody standing behind her and to her left in the same way that many people can "feel" when someone is staring at them without even looking. (The sensation of being watched is sometimes called "clairsentience," meaning clear feeling). Chloe was aware that clairsentience was a talent of hers, so she paid attention rather than becoming uncomfortable with the oddness of the experience.

She whispered aloud to the circle of people holding hands, "I sense a presence behind me and to my left. Are you Daniel?" Chloe waited patiently, know that a newly dead being might need to take some time figuring out how to respond to her; the response might come quite a bit later than if she were having a normal conversation with a living person. After about five minutes, Chloe began to hear an internal monologue in her head. Her perception was similar to when she heard her own voice in her head when she had normal thoughts but it was a man's voice, and she was used to being able to stop her own internal monologue for long periods of time during meditation. (Incidentally, this is another good reason to be well-practiced in meditation, so you can recognize when obtrusive thoughts are of a psychic nature rather than due to your own inexperience and inattentiveness.) At first, the male voice was difficult to make out, as if there were radio static or some other interference that didn't allow Chloe to understand the words.

"I hear a man's voice," Chloe said, letting her audience know that something was happening and in the process practicing the art of communicating well with the bereaved. Maggie broke the circle of hand-holding in order to grab the notebook and pen to write down that a man's voice had come through to the medium. As Chloe waited patiently, a few words began to come through. She heard him affirm that he was Daniel, and she relayed this information to his excited children. Chloe asked him aloud to share with her where his will was located, and explained respectfully that his children wanted to get such practical matters out of the way in order to heal as a family who missed him so much.

Chloe had divination tools in front of her, but she chose not to use them. Daniel seemed to want to speak with words instead of pictures, and none of these tools afforded him that opportunity. She felt Daniel's presence draw nearer to her but had difficulty making out the words. Since Chloe practiced channeling, she knew that Daniel wouldn't be able to "possess" her without her permission, but she wanted him to be able to speak through her so that the words might get across more clearly. She invited Daniel to channel his message through her more directly. Chloe concentrated on meditating again and allowed herself to relax even further in her trance, making room in her mind space for Daniel to enter her body and speak with her voice.

With eyes still closed, Chloe felt almost as if she was drifting to sleep as she meditated. She found herself going to that sacred place she had created on the astral plane, and spending quite some time there before returning to open her eyes. She found that she was still holding hands with those next to her in the circle, and she felt refreshed, like she had just awakened from a much-needed nap. She remembered Daniel's voice vaguely, but she felt very forgetful about what had just happened, as if it had been a dream. She noticed that Maggie had written some things down, so she readily confessed that she often did not remember much after channeling. She asked Maggie to recap what had happened so that anyone could ask additional questions if necessary.

Maggie related to the group how Chloe had spoken with her normal voice, but had used some of Daniel's speech mannerisms such as calling them "kiddos" as he used to do, even after they were adults, and making several jokes. Daniel had expressed his love and feelings of peace without regret, and told them that he had left his will underneath the keyboard of his computer. Such specificity was a relief, since Daniel's old home had been cluttered with his many hobbies. The surviving family members around the table felt content with their contact and had no further questions.

Chloe knew that there was no such thing as being too grounded at this point, her work being finished. She grounded herself before thanking everyone and closing the circle as well as afterward. She felt good that everyone in attendance seemed cheered by this connection with their beloved father and the feeling of security in the assurance of life after death they had all shared. Everyone was much more at ease and seemed to have bonded with each other more deeply after this experience. Richard gave Chloe a hug, and told her how much he appreciated having a psychic friend.

Channeling

Does the idea of being possessed fill you with dread or disbelief? Channeling probably isn't for you—it is the act of being the direct conduit for communications from a supernatural source. Luckily, this isn't a requirement to be a psychic. Rather than being the telephone itself, you might feel more comfortable being the person speaking on one end of it.

Channeling the dead can be a disturbing experience, especially if the person being channeled died in a violent way. A medium might experience channeling as living through the experience, seeing the frightening images, and potentially even feeling associated phantom pains. Though this does not cause lasting physical harm, it might be mentally and emotionally traumatizing to some. Consider carefully whether this is an activity you want to experience or avoid.

At the time of this writing, a client I was advising requested to ask an off-topic question about channeling. She wondered if as she works at developing her own psychic power, it was possible to become possessed. I explained that channeling was a difficult skill to learn. In our culture, it is extremely rare that an adult will accidentally channel anything and even more unlikely if that person is actively resisting possession. There are exceptions, of course, just as there are diseases which can turn the common cold into something nastier if one's immune system is compromised. At any rate, one shouldn't lose sleep worrying about it. If possession is something you wish to avoid, you will avoid it. On the other hand, it is something that can be developed through diligent effort if one truly desires it.

In my religion, a branch of British Traditional Wicca, we channel a goddess and a god regularly during group ritual. In this way, our deities can each speak directly through one person to the rest of the group. However, since this book isn't called *So You Want to Be a Prophet* or *So You Want to Be an Oracle*, I don't want to focus solely on the ability to have a deity speak through you.

After all, channeling in the context of psychic work is not a way to get to know the source of your psychic information more deeply—it is simply to convey information through spoken or written words or body language using yourself as a tool. When I was first learning to be possessed by and channel my goddess, I hoped it would be a way to bond with her. I imagined the experience to be like being able to sit and have tea with the divine. It was actually more like passing by her in a hallway as she went to speak through me and I went somewhere else, unable to really hear the message directly, having to wait until afterward to hear about it from my audience. Ironically, channeling is done through the psychic, but it serves others more than the psychic through whom it works.

Automatic Writing Channeling Exercise

Grab a pen and paper and choose a source you wish to channel through your hands. Your source can be a deity, spirit guide, or deceased person. For the greatest chance of success on your first try, choose somebody with whom you feel comfortable and who "speaks" to you in other ways. For example, if you have a close relationship with your god, you can try this first. If you have, say, a deceased grandmother who was talkative during life and who appears frequently in your dreams to give you advice, you can call upon her. In my personal experience, it is harder to channel deceased people who didn't speak my language, were babies too young to talk, or simply were not the chatty sort.

Ground and center yourself before working, and if you would like, you can cast a circle like the one given in the section on séances (p. 125). Request the presence of whomever you wish to summon, and tell yourself that you are going to begin channeling them through you by writing. You can begin by meditating receptively with your eyes closed, pen and paper in hand.

For some beginners and for many more practiced automatic writers, this is the time at which you will feel your hand begin to be compelled to move. You won't be forced to write. In fact, you can stop at any time or begin writing your own words whenever you wish. But if you allow automatic writing to occur, you will feel your hand being drawn to move. You can simply let it do so. Don't try to write words, and don't worry if it feels like your hand is just scribbling. I like to keep my eyes closed so my curiosity or expectations won't interfere with the process.

If after this time your hand hasn't felt compelled to move at all, you can try visualizing meeting with the entity in question in your sacred place on the astral plane. Try asking him or her to dictate a message to you. Automatic writing may take several tries before your hand moves at all and many more tries after that to get scribbles to resolve into legible handwriting. That being said, it is worth all that practice to have such an amazing tool to channel and record conversations with sources of psychic information.

Telepathy and Connecting with Others

As I sat down to write this chapter, I idly told my husband who was sitting nearby that I was thinking up ideas to write about telepathy. He put his hands up to his temples and stared at me intensely, rubbing his head and making a face. Then he asked, "how do you like my ideas?" His joke illustrates how silly it is to think that a psychic person is omniscient with an "all-access pass" to every thought in everyone's head. Telepathy can be quite useful, however.

Imagine lovers separated by a great distance. Perhaps one is a young man sent off to war, unable to send much communication in order to preserve his own safety. His young wife is pregnant with his child and misses him deeply. Wouldn't it be wonderful if they could be linked through their minds in a psychic way so he could be there mentally at the birth of their child or so she could be there mentally if he should die in battle to hear his last words to her and their baby? A telepathic connection makes that possible.

Earlier you learned that you can connect with another willing person through dreams. Any connection to another person's mind is telepathy. Doing so while dreaming is a good way to start; eventually you can incorporate meditation sessions so you can connect during your waking time as well. With frequent practice between two enthusiastic partners, this connection can strengthen such that you have brief flashes of connection without even trying. You may have accidentally experienced dream connections in the past or waking flashes of connection, especially with a close family member, such as a mother sensing when a daughter is in danger.

The benefits are many, especially over a distance as in the example of the soldier above. Another more common case is two lovers separated over a distance due to going to different colleges in different states. The connection can be helpful even if you are physically close to the person, as in the example of the mother sensing when her daughter is in danger. An intuitive sense about the imminent danger of a loved one happened often with my own mother even in minor situations of my own emotional distress. I remember one instance when my friend's older brother was frightening us, and my mom immediately called her house sensing that I needed her. Though this scenario often happens naturally, it is important to gain permission at the very least before attempting telepathy. Active participation from your partner is best.

If the two of you are physically close, increasing the time you spend together connecting on a deep level can naturally bring about a psychic connection. If you are distant, focus on connecting with each other through your different senses—sometimes that will allow your psychic sense to pick up to a greater degree as well. Let me give an example using lovers separated due to college, since it is a common situation among my clients. Read the section on dreams in chapter 2 for more information on how to dream with someone. In the following example are some of the recommendations I often make for such clients in this situation.

Nineteen-year-old Javon was excited to be moving away from home and into the dorm rooms at a college six hundred miles away from his home town. Unfortunately, he would also be leaving behind his high school sweetheart, Annie, whom he had known since childhood. They were both committed to maintaining a long term relationship, and he planned to propose to her when he finished school in four years. However, it was difficult—the trip to visit her was long and he couldn't afford to do it very often. Since Annie was waiting tables for a living, she didn't have the money to make the journey very often either. Luckily, they both believed in psychic connections, and worked out a plan to connect psychically with one another to deepen their relationship during their time apart.

In his first week, having moved into the dormitory, Javon worked to establish a connection with Annie through each of his senses. He had eggplant parmigiana for dinner, the meal they shared during prom; it always reminded him of her. For dessert, he had some cookies Annie baked and mailed to him in a care package. As he finished getting ready for bed, the phone rang. Annie's familiar voice was on the other end. She had arranged to go to bed at the same time, so they chatted a while about the day and about how they looked forward to meeting in their dreams.

As the conversation wound to a close, they confirmed their love once again, and he smiled at her photograph on the wall before switching off the light and snuggling up close to a teddy bear that wore her favorite t-shirt. (Yes, guys can have stuffed animals, too!) The teddy still smelled of her perfume, and he breathed it in deeply as he visualized the park in which they first met. Tonight they planned to meet underneath a tree in their dreams.

Behind his closed eyes, Javon visualized every aspect of the place he remembered. He could smell the blossoms and feel the bark of the tree under the palm of his hand. He heard the birds chirping. The wind picked up and moved the leaves of the tree, fanning his cheeks. As his dorm room melted away under the heaviness of sleep, he saw a figure approaching in the distance. He recognized that the person he saw was Annie, and as she approached, flushed with excitement, he knew that they were truly together on the astral plane.

In the above story, the two people involved worked hard to improve their connection in the same way a mother and her child might, by connecting with the different senses and thinking about each other. Building a bridge of caring between two people is a purposeful yet organic way to grow a psychic link so the two of you can communicate in many ways. With this new skill, if Javon has a difficult day at school—perhaps after failing an exam—Annie might sense his sadness and give him a phone call that cheers him up at just the right moment.

If you and a friend wish to toy with psychic linking, you could try Zener cards (see chapter 4). The 5-to-1 ratio should skew in favor of more correct answers the deeper the connection you make with your partner and the more you practice.

In order to test your clairvoyance, you could simply try to visualize in your mind's eye the image on the actual card before you turn it over or before it is shown to you, or an image of what was on a card that has been drawn in another location. In order to test telepathy, however, one partner concentrates on an image on a card without revealing it yet to the other person, the other partner is supposed to attempt to sense the information directly from his or her partner's mind. Even though this is done obviously with the consent of the other person, it strays farther into the realm of pure "mind reading" than the psychic connection between the couple in this chapter's story. As such, telepathy might be less useful in everyday life since one can just speak aloud one's thoughts instead of going through all the work involved to establish a psychic connection. Talking to communicate is much easier on the brain. However, telepathy might be a fun exercise for two friends to do together.

One might be tempted to use telepathy on a subject who has not yet consented. For example, if a woman has a crush on a male coworker, she might wish to attempt to sense whether he likes her as well by reading his mind. Or, a teenager with an enemy who makes fun of her in class might wish to appear in the bully's dreams to scare her out of continuing the harassment. This non-consensual telepathy is ill-advised on ethical grounds, not to mention that it probably wouldn't work at all.

Controlling the mind of another in a negative way is unethical. My own personal morals about this stems from my spiritual belief that the energies I send out into the universe will return to me. The return of those energies I send out has operated in my own life very much like a natural law. Have you ever been so angry at somebody, such as a parent, you stared daggers at them all day long, wishing they would spill their coffee or just that something in their life would get harder? Chances are that nothing bad happened but you worsened your own mood and probably gave yourself a whopping headache to boot. The headache is your own projected anger returning to you.

Psychic linking is not something I invented; it can happen naturally as in the example of a mother sensing when her daughter is in danger. When emotions are the messages being conveyed from one person to a psychic, that psychic is often called an "empath." Some people are natural empaths with the proclivity to attempt to try telepathy, perhaps without even knowing it. Everyone has similarly automatic defenses against such attempts; whether somebody believes in psychic abilities or not doesn't matter, the defense is still there.

Psychic defense is similar to our immune system's natural defense against germs. Even if you don't believe in or are unaware of viruses, your body will still create antibodies and mount a defense when one enters your system. Thus, even the most unsuspecting of victims can skillfully repel your psychic attack and land you with the consequences of it sitting squarely in your lap. Don't waste your time attempting such antics. Instead, work out your differences with people in a more direct way. My most frequent answer to clients who ask me how they can figure out whether somebody likes them is to simply ask the person directly.

....

Homework

Solo

Try the automatic writing exercise provided in this chapter. Automatic writing is a form of channeling you can do alone because you can be your own note-taker. Automatic writing is a good skill to have to help you get into the channeling frame of mind quickly and with ease. Automatic writing is also a good substitute for times when a séance is not necessary or would be inappropriate. For example if you wish to speak to a deceased person about a very personal and private manner, or if you don't think there are any other people who can or should respectfully participate, perhaps a séance is not the best idea.

Another practical reason to use automatic writing as a beginner is that you're keeping your records as you go, so it can be especially useful for tracking your progress and analyzing symbols in the same manner you would with a dream journal. Start practicing automatic writing on your own so you can have this skill as yet another tool under your belt during your psychic readings. Before you try automatic writing, make sure you've worked on the homework in chapter 2 so you are familiar with grounding and meditation. Because automatic writing must be performed after a trance state has been achieved, grounding must be done adequately—especially afterward.

With a Partner

Hopefully by now you've attempted to dream with someone as in the homework in chapter 2 and you've made some cards with a partner to test your ESP, as in chapter 4. If either of those exercises haven't worked for you yet, the additional information in this chapter should help you make another attempt. Try dreaming with someone again and test your clairvoyant ESP with a partner once more.

If you've succeeded at calling upon deceased ancestors and relative strangers during dreams, meditation, and divination and you're feeling especially ambitious, you can make it a goal to attempt a séance. Use compassion when choosing the deceased you wish to summon for your séance, and make sure that the bereaved will not be hindered in their grieving process by selecting a deceased person who has passed too recently.

6 How to Convey Messages

Imagine you had a dream in which you saw something awful happen to somebody you didn't know. Imagine that the dream was so vivid and seemed so meaningful that it shocked you awake. Perhaps you saw a woman get into a red car and run a red light just in time to be hit by a truck. As you awake to the terror of grinding metal and a scene so intensely violent that you are certain she would have been seriously injured (if not killed), I would hope you would record such a dream in your journal for further analysis.

Now imagine that as you continued on your day, you went to the grocery store and were shocked to see the woman from your dream heading to a red car in the parking lot. To your horror, you realize the intersection from your dream is right outside the parking lot. Would you approach this stranger and attempt to warn her, just in case the dream was not just a symbol? What if the person in your dream was your boss or a coworker? What if it was a very good friend or your mother? Is there any right way to share this sort of frightening message?

Each person might answer this question differently. I personally always get permission before sharing a psychic message with anyone. Some people find it rude or even unethical to read someone without permission, but often you might find that *not* reading people is impossible. In such cases, you must then decide whether and how to convey the messages you receive. When you are approached for a psychic reading, you'll find that reading for somebody else is quite different than reading for yourself. Even the most skilled psychic might be terrible at translating the messages he or she receives into something that makes sense and can be relayed to another person successfully.

In addition to being careful about what might be a symbol or even just your imagination (versus what might be the real message), you must also deliver it in a coherent and tactful way. Sometimes this might be under the extreme pressure of what you perceive as the other person's expectations, especially if you feel like you are being too slow or too general with your psychic reading or if you are charging a client for the privilege of working with you. No matter how you look at this, performing psychic readings for other people is a skill developed with practice—and that includes some mistakes along the way.

Psychic Reading for a Purpose

Have you ever played with a Magic 8-Ball? The Magic 8-Ball toy can be pretty fun for fortune telling. Ask it a question, and receive an answer in the form of "yes" or "no" or a similar brief response. The Magic 8-Ball can be an endless source of entertainment for teenage girls asking whether so-and-so has a crush on someone, or whether fame and fortune will be forthcoming someday. But there are obvious limitations to the Magic 8-Ball's answers, even if they were always mystically correct. Can you imagine asking a Magic 8-Ball how to solve your marital difficulties, or what you could do in order to best move through the grief of the death of a parent? The best advice it could possibly come up with is to say: "Cannot predict now." Psychic readings often have an important purpose behind them, and this is why people turn to the help of a compassionate and skillful psychic to advise them, rather than the Magic 8-Ball.

If you choose to take the plunge and be a psychic for other people as well as for yourself, you will most likely run into people who desire psychic readings. When they wish to use them for help in their lives, such people will without a doubt have a topic in mind or a question they would love answered, as opposed to those merely seeking entertainment. As I explore the tricky assortment of skills used in performing a psychic reading for another, I will take a look at several common purposes for readings and give you examples. First I will show how psychic readings might go horribly wrong, and then show how you might be able to have a more successful experience.

Love

Shelly was in the break room at her job, reading through *So You Want to Be a Psychic Intuitive?*, every once in a while glancing at the clock to wait out the last fifteen minutes before it was time to get back to work. The peacefulness of her alone time was suddenly broken as her coworker, Trudy, shoved the door open so hard that it thudded heavily against the rubber stopper and broke all hope of concentration. "I've had it with dating!" Trudy said as she plopped down in a chair at Shelly's table with a huff.

"Remember how I just started going out with that guy, Don?" Trudy didn't pause for Shelly's acknowledgment, which was merciful since Shelly could never keep up with the ups and downs of Trudy's love life. "Well, he stood me up, just after I was starting to fall for him! I've had it with all this garbage. Say, you're a psychic, right? Tell me who it is that I'm going to marry forever, and when that will happen. I want his name and the place and day I'll meet him, so that I can stop wasting my time!" Shelly stared back at Trudy's expectant eyes for several seconds before she realized that Trudy wanted all that information right at that moment. The clock said there were only ten more minutes left of her break. She carefully set down her book.

Shelly closed her eyes and tried to concentrate, but unlike meditating at home, her mind was already becoming far too cluttered with worries about producing satisfactory results for Trudy. She skipped through the steps of her meditation so fast that she wasn't sure whether she was truly in a trance or simply pushing herself to imagine what she wanted. The buzzing sound of the soda machine kept distracting her from her work, and she found herself wondering if Trudy thought she was taking too long. Stressful thoughts made the period of time stretch out even longer. Shelly saw a vision of Trudy surrounded by several men, but when she spoke that out loud, Trudy grew even more impatient. "But which one will I marry?" Shelly tried to focus on the varied expressions the men had, to try to find a clue, but Trudy was still asking questions. "When will I marry him? What is his name?"

Frustrated, Shelly attempted to describe the physical characteristics of the man sitting next to Trudy in her mind's eye, but when she took a peek at Trudy's actual face, she could see boredom. Shelly was thinking far more about Trudy's reaction to the reading than about the process of the reading itself. She could feel herself becoming more and more self-conscious as the seconds ticked by, and she wanted nothing more than to end the reading. Hurriedly, Shelly just blurted the first date and name that popped into her head and Trudy hopped up happily and left the room. Shelly didn't feel quite so satisfied. She knew her answers had been mere wild guesses, and she felt they weren't correct at all. Trudy wouldn't be very happy when her hopes didn't come to pass. Shelly quickly rose to return to work.

She was already a minute late, and she felt a bit nauseated and dizzy from not grounding properly. Shelly knew that today was going to be a long day.

Love is definitely the most popular subject amongst my clients, and the above story is just one example of how a reading with a genuine psychic may go horribly awry and produce less-than-genuine results. Love is difficult; there's just no way to make relationships easy. The perfect man or woman is not going to appear out of nowhere. Even if such a miracle were to occur, negotiating a lifelong relationship is not going to always mean smooth sailing—especially if you care for each other. So how can you satisfy a client, friend, or relative when their requested topic is love?

You'll go a long way towards the goal of a happy, in-formed client if you can manage expectations right off the bat. Since people are passionate about love, it can be challenging to do this type of reading tactfully. I find that the best way to do this is to re-frame the person's questions. Start off by remembering your goals. Why do you want to be a psychic? If it is because you wish to help people rather than to just give instant responses that relieve them from having to think about the issue, you will need to stay firm when asked questions you cannot or do not wish to attempt to answer. Rephrase the question in order to help the other person achieve the outcome he or she truly desires. The re-phrased question would ask what the person should do in order to increase the likelihood of finding love according to the specifications he or she wishes. If a person wishes to have a healthy love relationship, no name, date, or even physical description will magically bring it about.

The confusion caused by answers that are too concrete is sort of like that caused by giving a short yes or no answer where an essay response is required. I am reminded of the novel *The Hitchhiker's Guide to the Galaxy*, wherein the answer to "life, the universe, and everything" was said to be 42. That isn't very helpful, or even comprehensible, no matter how accurate it may be. A search had to be embarked upon to find the "question" in that case, and I suggest you start out with the right question to save you all some trouble. Let's re-examine the story of the botched love reading.

Asking a Question

Shelly prepared her home for a guest, having told coworker Trudy that the break room was neither the time nor the place for a serious psychic reading. Here on her home turf, Shelly could arrange for adequate time for her psychic reading and eliminate potential sources of interruption. As soon as Trudy arrived Shelly was instantly barraged with the same questions she had heard before, but this time she had some questions of her own. What did Trudy want her love life to look like? Trudy was feeling lonely and hoped to end a long dry spell with love as soon as possible with a marriage that would last forever.

Her hopes that marriage would happen quickly were what caused Trudy to ask when she would meet her future spouse, rather than a desire to actually mark her calendar.

So Shelly asked Trudy's permission to change her question to "What can Trudy do in order to meet a successful marriage potential within the next year?" Upon further questioning by Shelly, she discovered that Trudy's desire for a name and physical description came from her concern that she would miss the right man or waste time with the wrong man. Shelly pointed out that hard-learned lessons are anything but a waste of time. Now with Trudy's permission, Shelly changed those questions to "How will Trudy know that she is on the right track with her relationships" and "How can Trudy make the best out of the ups and downs of dating?"

Feeling relaxed and confident in her hopes to help Trudy in her journey to find love, Shelly grounded and centered herself before allowing time to drop deep into meditation and slowly go to her sacred place on the astral plane to look for answers to the questions she and Trudy had formed together. She saw Trudy surrounded by family and friends who held up mirrors to her smiling face as she accepted flowers and chocolates from several men...and then frowned and cautiously bade several of them to leave.

Returning to a more aware state of consciousness, Shelly admitted to Trudy that she might have to make a few mistakes before she found the right partner for her. She told her that her state of happiness or sadness could be closely monitored to observe whether she was with somebody who was treating her in the manner she deserved. She mentioned that she had seen Trudy's mother and best friend in the vision, and said that they could easily advise Trudy as to whether she was being her happy self if Trudy lost touch with how her love life really was affecting her feelings. Finally, Shelly described a man who hadn't been rejected in the vision, with the caveat that he might be only a symbolic representation, so she didn't want Trudy to be close-minded towards someone who didn't fit the description exactly but who everyone else could see made her happy. Trudy felt a little more confident in her ability to assess men, and was happy to know that she could afford to be choosy. Though she still wished dating were easier, she felt a renewed sense of determination to tackle the world with other loved ones by her side.

Disappointment starts with unreasonable ideas about how time spent with a psychic will go. As you can see from the story above, managing expectations might be a little disappointing to a person at the start of a session but not as much if you dig deeper for the true reasons for their original questions. Start understanding expectations by listening. After you're done addressing the person's real needs, you'll find that they will often feel better having been empowered than if they had received instant answers that might misinterpret or oversimplify how life really works. Don't be afraid to be a practical psychic.

Money

Ronnie was overjoyed to have his first paying client as a professional psychic. He had just set up a storefront in a strip mall near his home and was embarking on what he hoped would be a fulfilling career as a trusted advisor. His client called early that day on the telephone, asking if Ronnie could set a same-day appointment to help with some financial questions. He eagerly agreed and was thrilled when she arrived at the appointed time. His client was a no-nonsense-looking woman named Barbara, who handed over her money without fuss and got right down to business, taking out a notebook upon which she had written her questions, and preparing to take notes.

Barbara had a couple of questions that revolved around money. Her first was about whether she should invest in short-term stocks. Her second question was regarding how to minimize money loss during her divorce proceedings. Ronnie took out his trusty pendulum to ask it to show him what a "yes" answer would look like. As he dangled it from his hand, it moved in a clockwise circle. He asked it to show him what a "no" answer would look like, and it waved back and forth. Ronnie asked "should Barbara invest in stock trading?" The pendulum immediately swung in an affirmative circle and he and Barbara exchanged a smile. She wrote down the answer and was ready for her next question to be addressed.

For her next question, Ronnie took out his crystal ball to look for a clairvoyant answer. As he turned the quartz crystal sphere in his hand, the small imperfections inside of it glinted in the light and shifted in front of his eyes like clouds in the sky. He froze as he spotted a meaningful shape. The occlusions inside the crystal formed something that looked exactly like a door with a heavy padlock. No matter how he turned the crystal, he couldn't see anything but that locked door. Ronnie decided it meant that Barbara should hide her assets from her husband to prevent him from being able to obtain them. Barbara wrote this down and thanked Ronnie profusely, handing him a hefty tip that made him feel proud.

That proud feeling lasted nearly a month until Ronnie found an extremely frightening letter in his mailbox. The letter was from Barbara's attorney, stating that she had taken his advice and had lost a lot of money on the stock market. She had also gotten into plenty of legal trouble for fraud when she made some mistakes trying to hide her husband's own money from him. Ronnie realized that he didn't have liability insurance to cover this; he could lose his business, his home, and his life's savings over this.

We could all use a little more money in our lives. However, performing a psychic reading on money matters can be troublesome. I often run into the same problems encountered in love readings. Clients ask for precise numbers and dates when their true desire is simply to provide for themselves and their families. Questions often need to be rephrased, but the additional point needs to be made that there is no way to guarantee money from a psychic reading. If there were, we would all be filthy rich psychics, too busy playing on our yachts in some tropical paradise to help our clients. Without this important disclaimer, you might find yourself leading a person on who might be very litigious indeed. Let's re-imagine the terrifying scenario above in a better way.

When Ronnie received his first client appointment phone call he was excited, but he didn't let his excitement get the better of him. He heard her drop the word "financial" with regard to her questions, and he wanted to make sure she had reasonable expectations before having her travel all the way out to see him. "Do you feel comfortable sharing your questions with me now, so I can make sure I can serve you best?" She was only too happy to tell him about what she planned to ask. Ronnie frowned as he listened.

"Well first of all," he explained, "I'm not a financial advisor, nor am I a lawyer. So I'm not sufficiently qualified to answer either of those questions without your having first consulted a financial planner and an attorney." Ronnie worried that he was turning away his very first client, but the woman on the other end didn't seem fazed by his requirements. She explained that she had been contemplating the wisdom of seeing those professionals anyway, and asked if she could make an appointment for next week instead of later that day. Ronnie did so gladly, saying he looked forward to helping her.

The following week, Barbara showed up right on time. Ronnie asked her if her questions had changed since they had last spoken. Barbara nodded cheerfully, explaining that her financial planner had created a plan for her that involved many investments in order to create a diverse and stable portfolio. Since a few of them were up to chance, she had brought in a couple of options her financial planner had left up to her discretion. She asked Ronnie to help her choose between two stock options that had already been approved by her other professional. The pendulum easily indicated which one should be chosen.

She wrote down the stock that the pendulum indicated as Ronnie asked her what her second question was. She looked a little bashful and said, "actually, I don't need to ask that question anymore. My attorney already has established ways to get through a divorce with the least amount of financial loss possible, so I won't be needing your help with that one. But thank you anyway." She gave Ronnie a generous tip. A few months later, he received a very friendly phone call from Barbara letting him know that he had helped her make the right decision and that she would be sending him a gift for the holidays.

Though the illustrations may be a bit exaggerated, you can see in the examples that drawing a line between what you can and cannot do is good not only for your clients, but for you as well. Boundaries keep you safe from potential anger, resentment, or legal action if your signs are misinterpreted, and they help keep you in your rightful place as a psychic and not another kind of professional. I believe a psychic can be a helpful part of a team of other professionals but is not a replacement for qualified financial, legal, or medical advice. Don't be afraid to draw the line and tell people what you won't do. Chances are they'll find something you *can* do and love you for that.

Talking to the Dead

Having a conversation with somebody who has crossed over can be bittersweet and can make you feel very important. But for many psychics, they don't just come through at specified psychic mediumship sittings. As hard as it is to be sensitive to the bereaved during such arranged circumstances, it can be even harder when a ghost seems to come tearing out of the void when you are not conducting a séance. They usually want to share a disturbing message you then feel compelled to pass on to somebody who knew the person during his or her lifetime. As in the case of receiving a message about somebody's life being in danger, if you randomly approach someone with a message from a dead relative, you'll be seen as tacky at best. Sometimes there just isn't a right way to do it, but here is a good example of the wrong way.

Laura saw dead people. Seeing dead people might be scary in a movie, but to her it was something she was used to. Laura's ability was actually more annoying than scary, especially when they kept her up at night. So when she listened idly to the ghost of a teenage girl whispering urgently at her one morning as she chewed her cereal, an idea suddenly hit her. The teenaged ghost had just said a name that sounded quite familiar. She had heard about this girl on television: her parents had been shown on the nightly news, crying about their hopes for her safe return after she had disappeared from a local campus.

Excited, Laura hopped up to find out how to contact those parents. Perhaps solving this case was the reason she had been plagued with these meddlesome ghosts her entire life. Maybe this contact meant that she had been destined for fame this entire time. Otherwise the girl wouldn't have come to her at all. Feeling like fate had led her to this point, Laura called a couple of news stations before contacting the parents of the teenage girl, announcing to the media that she was there to be their psychic investigator.

Laura then called the mother and immediately rattled off information the girl had shared with her. She told her that the young girl had gotten blind drunk and had wandered off into a field with a young man who subsequently hit her over the head with an object and had raped her. Presented with this graphic vision of violence, the astounded mother sobbed uncontrollably on the other end of the telephone, begging Laura to tell her at least that her daughter was happy now that she was on the other side. Laura paused to listen to the ghost a moment. "Actually, she isn't happy at all," Laura replied, trying to be honest, "because she says that you never accepted the fact that she was a lesbian, and so she wasn't really talking to you at the time of her death." There was an audible click as the mother hung up the phone.

Laura felt bad about hurting the woman's feelings, but she hoped that she would be vindicated when the police searched the local farm fields and discovered the girl's body. The news teams she had notified called her back, and she asked them if they had heard about what the police had found with her information. To Laura's surprise, the news teams indicated that the parents of the girl never shared her information with the police and instead thought Laura was harassing them, perhaps trying to swindle money from desperate people. They wanted to know how Laura slept at night.

Trying to show that she was telling the truth, Laura called the police emergency line to tell them where to look for the girl's body, but her instructions were vague; instead she received a rather scary lecture from the dispatcher on how she could be arrested for wasting valuable police time. The next week, Laura was in the papers as a "fraudulent" psychic who preyed on victims.

As this story indicates, your motives can easily be misunderstood when you are a psychic, particularly when grief is involved. Misunderstandings are to be expected due to an early stage of grief processing. Even if you hear dead people, ghosts aren't to be blindly obeyed. Think of the reasons why you might be sharing the information and the desired outcome. Sharing more than needed might cause more harm than good. Here's a more gentle route the psychic in my story could have taken.

Listening carefully to the ghost's message, Laura wrote down all the details that might be factual. She was able to get some precise names of people as well as some physical descriptions. Laura looked up and called the police's non-emergency tip hotline. She immediately confessed she was a psychic medium who wanted to give some quickly verifiable facts and volunteered to try to get more information if requested. She related her notes to the person on the line, gave them her own name and number, and ending with a thank-you, was done for the day. She hoped she had done the right thing.

A couple of hours later, she was contacted by a member of the police force who had verified her facts. He asked if she would come into the station to help them a little further. Upon arriving, Laura was asked if she could provide a more clear description of where the body could be found. Laura asked to hold one of the girl's belongings if possible. They handed her a backpack of the girl's that had been found on campus. Upon clutching the backpack, Laura again was able to hear the voice of the ghost who appeared by her side. Laura gave the police some street names and a description of the farm near the field in which the girl's body lay. She was then thanked and she hurried home.

After the case was solved with the help of Laura's information, the parents of the girl telephoned Laura to thank her personally. When the mother asked Laura to tell her whether her daughter was happy on the other side, Laura said, "Are you sure you're ready to hear such messages? Sometimes words from the other side can be pretty raw and powerful, and they might hinder the grieving process if heard at the wrong time." The mother confessed that she wasn't really ready for an in-depth psychic message from her daughter at the time and thanked Laura again before letting her go. Laura was happy she had made a difference in this case.

Connecting with the Living

You've already been warned frequently throughout this book not to try to use telepathy with somebody without his or her permission, because it is unlikely to work due to everyone's natural psychic defenses and also because it's just not nice. We work with the energy of those around us all the time without them knowing it, however. Energy working is a natural part of how people operate. Just like we inhale air other people have already exhaled, the energies are out there in the world for us to read without harming others in the same way that one can look up at the sky to read weather signs if it looks like rain. The following story will show some consequences of reading that energy.

Lewis was one of those people who had a lot of friends and acquaintances. Though he lived in a pretty large suburb, it had a small-town feel where everyone knew everybody else. When he wasn't keeping up with his various social circles, he was online using social networks to keep up with friends near and far. Naturally, everybody in town knew he was the go-to psychic for readings that were both fun and informative. Some of his friends even seemed rather addicted.

Rebecca, for instance, was a long-time friend and former coworker who was now friends with Lewis' sister as well. They often hung out together on Friday nights at a local pub and sometimes came home as a group for tarot readings that went on late into the night. Rebecca tended to have more readings than anyone else, often asking about her screwy relationship with her mother or her various spats with mutual friends.

Whenever Rebecca had a boyfriend, he was constantly a topic for her readings. Her latest beau, Greg, sometimes came out to the pub with them and obligingly listened back at Lewis's house as Rebecca asked question after question about their relationship. He thought tarot readings were harmless fun but didn't really believe in them.

One weekend, Rebecca and Greg had a falling out. She came to Lewis's house crying and saying that Greg wanted to spend more time with her, but she had so many other social and work obligations that it was next to impossible. He was considering breaking up with her for someone who could devote more attention to him. Rebecca knew that Lewis had talked about connecting with others through telepathy, so Rebecca wanted advice and help.

Lewis suggested that perhaps Greg and Rebecca could connect more with each other in their dreams if they wanted. Rebecca thought this was a splendid idea, and listened with rapt attention while Lewis explained to her how to meditate and what she and Greg should do in order to attempt to have dreams about one another. "Look, you're friends of both of us," Rebecca said carefully, "would you also come to join us in our dreams to help us reconnect?" Lewis didn't see why not; he wanted happiness for both of them. He agreed that he would attempt to dream about them as well, and they could all three get together to trade notes the following day.

That night, Lewis meditated upon Greg and Rebecca before bed, but he did not dream of them. The next morning, he received a shocking phone call from Greg. "Rebecca told me that she is getting you to use your imaginary powers to try to force me to love her again, but it's not going to work. Leave me alone, I'm through with her after all of this!" Greg hung up on Lewis, who felt very foolish now for not getting Greg's permission directly since obviously Rebecca had been less than truthful. But Lewis's humiliation didn't stop there. Word spread quickly and Lewis was soon no longer known as that cool guy who does tarot readings, but instead as that creepy dude who thinks he has psychic powers to force people to do stuff. He was unable to find a date in town for quite some time.

In the above example you can see where the line was drawn for one particular person. Some people are insulted if they find out you ever performed a reading on them without their permission. Avoiding dream work with third parties entirely may be wise, and you could change the question in readings to focus more on the second party and not the third. So for example, if the client in the story had asked whether her ex-boyfriend would choose to get back together with her, the psychic could instead ask what she could do in order to maximize her chances of letting him get back together with her, if that is what he ultimately chose for himself. However, since the people in the above case were supposedly still together when the client went overboard with her attempted solution, I would have asked the couple to come in together. Here's an example of how to orchestrate such a situation.

As Rebecca sobbed about her problems with Greg, Lewis realized that working together in dreams might solve their problem of not seeing much of each other during their waking days, but he was unsure of how to teach Greg to do that without doing so directly. He asked Rebecca if she would like to invite Greg to try such a solution and if they would come over together. Rebecca agreed and asked if Lewis would perform a tarot reading on whether Greg would be open to the idea. Remembering that Greg wasn't a huge fan of tarot readings, Lewis suggested they save the readings for when the two of them came in together.

When Rebecca and Greg arrived at Lewis's house at the appointed time, he started out by explaining the basics of dream working, since he knew Greg was inexperienced with psychic phenomena. He also explained how and why to meditate before they began, emphasizing to Greg that at the very least, meditation was a healthy practice. Lewis guided both of them through some controlled breathing and relaxation of muscles, and then through basic visualization of things in the room, especially each other. Then

Lewis spoke of the astral realm and asked each to visualize their ideal place of relaxation. He gave them some silent time to work on that visualization. Afterwards, he asked them to slowly come back to the shared reality and asked if either of them would like to share something about their astral space.

Feeling relaxed and rejuvenated, Greg shared what he had seen in his mind's eye and admitted that it was fun, whether or not it was real. Rebecca told him about her astral space and they agreed to attempt to meet each other on the astral plane that night in their dreams. When Rebecca asked if Lewis would perform a tarot card reading to see if their relationship would succeed, Lewis asked if they would rather have a reading on what each of them could do in order to help resolve their relationship problems in the best way possible for both of them. To that, each heartily agreed.

As you become a psychic, you'll see a lot of situations in which people ask primarily about other people rather than themselves. Don't fall into the trap of thinking that people see you as a mind reader who can finally prevent them from having to ask those pesky hard questions of their lovers, or who really only want you to gossip about coworkers or who want you as a listening ear while they rant about their family. A need for negative venting isn't always the case, and you'll find that involving couples or groups in psychic readings can be a powerful way to solve problems.

Past Lives

I chose to save examples on the topic of past lives for last because there are many who, although they believe in psychics, don't believe in past lives or have no interest in them at all. A past life can also be a notoriously difficult subject to attempt to convey to another person. Many past lives may contribute to a mixed-up psychic reading, or there might be an aspect of a past life that can lead the psychic reader down an interesting path of discussion that may not be useful to the client at all, leaving the person feeling confused and wondering if you're a nutcase. Take this example of a psychic falling down the wrong rabbit hole, for instance.

Anna was a psychic who firmly believed in the existence of past lives. In fact, she was already aware of at least a dozen of her own past lives, which she had experienced firsthand in meditative visions and explored further using her new skills with tarot cards as a tool. However, she was still very nervous when a good friend of hers asked if she would perform a past-life reading on her. After all, Anna's encounters with her own past lives had been in the first person, so she was feeling a little anxious about how to figure out the past life of someone else. Figuring out a past life was out of her comfort zone. After all, she could only be herself in past lives on the astral plane—not somebody else.

Anna's friend Ellie invited Anna to her house in order to have the psychic reading performed before dinner. She was quite excited about it and had been thinking about a particular past life of hers, but wanted to find out more information about it using Anna's special talents and skills. When Anna came in the door, Ellie was already bubbling about the things she had already felt or known about a specific past life that she hoped would come up in the psychic reading. She wondered if this past life somehow related to her attempts in this life to become a teacher. There were so many details that Anna was finding it hard to follow along.

Feeling a little awkward about using her tarot cards with somebody else, Anna asked Ellie to shuffle the cards, and hoped that she could remember the meanings. When she performed readings for herself with the tarot cards, she always had her book with open in front of her so she could work with the traditional meanings as well as her own feelings about each card. She decided to only use one card, so as to limit the reading and her discomfort.

She drew the King of Swords and stared at it, trying to remember what was on that page in her book. She felt her mind go blank and panicked. "Maybe you were a king in a past life?" Anna was guessing—they both knew it. Ellie tried to hide her disappointment with a smile. She complimented Anna on how pretty the tarot card was and thanked her for taking the time to show her how it worked. She changed the subject by going to set the table.

In the above story, the psychic did the right thing by choosing a sympathetic friend to try out her new tarot skills. Trying unfamiliar forms of divination on others is okay. However, Anna made the common mistake in this type of reading of focusing on past life's physical form and occupation. While that's what people want to know on television and in the movies, I rarely find that attitude outside of a party atmosphere.

In my experience, those who want a past-life reading do so because they're already practically obsessed with one of their past lives due to its influence continuously cropping up in their current life. I have clients who have frequent dreams about a specific past life, and who find themselves drawn to and talented with skills (such as knitting) that feel like they were connected to a prior time. Some of my clients resonated with specific places after traveling there, and just "knew" that they had spent significant time there during a previous life.

In such cases, getting wrapped up with names and occupations isn't the best use of your psychic abilities. The purpose and outcome of such a psychic reading might be improved by exploring why the connection with that life remains. Perhaps there is a life lesson that was not properly learned in that past life, and now this life is touching on that same lesson, tugging at the person's soul. In this example, I want to show what might happen if you work in a partnership with another person during a psychic reading. The following method may not be the best choice for a skeptic who fears a cold reading scam, but it can be a helpful method of reading for others who are friends or loved ones who trust you and are intuitive themselves.

Anna listened carefully to what Ellie was telling her about the past life in question, which was difficult due to Ellie's fast-talking enthusiasm. She often had to ask questions herself in order to get the right time frame and sequence of events in her mind. Ellie had obviously already done a lot of work not only in her dreams but with external research on the time period and people involved as well. She concluded her explanation with the hopes that she could figure out what karmic lesson from that past life was still nagging at her today.

Admitting that she was still learning how to use tarot cards, Anna pulled out her book along with her deck of cards and smiled as she asked Ellie to bear with her. She laid out four cards: one to represent Ellie's physical form in that past life, one to represent her mental state and actions taken, and one to represent her spiritual achievements. The final card represented a lesson carrying over or linking Ellie's past life to her present one. As she drew the cards, she took time looking at each one before opening her tarot book. She asked Ellie to look at them as well. "What would this picture mean to you with relation to that life?"

The card representing her mind in that past life was the King of Swords, which in Anna's particular tarot deck depicted a man riding a horse. Ellie frowned thoughtfully at the card. "Actually, that does remind me of my work in the dreams. I was a messenger, and often carried words on horseback." Anna consulted her book and confirmed that the suit of Swords often represented communications like what Ellie was talking about. In fact, the final (connecting) card was the Three of Swords showing the trio of blades stabbing a heart. Anna and Ellie both agreed that it looked like she hadn't done well with communication in that past life! They spent the rest of the time before dinner talking about how teaching was a form of sharing a message and how she continues to be drawn to that occupation in this life. To Ellie, the reading confirmed that she was on the right career path to enrich her life spiritually.

Reading for Others

Letting other people rely on you for a psychic message can be empowering. It can also be rewarding to be the person who connects another person with his or her own intuitive power. Don't be afraid to share your own thinking process with friends when you read for them, even if it underscores the fact that you aren't omniscient. Not knowing what you don't know is okay. You can help build an understanding with another person. Perhaps there is a reason this particular person came to you as his or her psychic, as opposed to going to someone that you feel is better or more practiced at the craft.

ASKING DIFFICULT QUESTIONS EXERCISE

Before you begin reading for someone else, I think it is important that you put yourself in their shoes. Going to a psychic can be frightening, especially if the person has the wrong idea about your capabilities. Imagine meeting somebody that you thought knew everything about you, and everything that was ever going to happen to you. You might feel humble and a little worried that you were going to hear something bad.

Now, I want you to think about a question to which you wouldn't want to hear the answer, and think about how you might change that question to make it more useful and comfortable to answer. Why wouldn't you want to hear the answer? What is the true purpose for the question? A questioning thought process may help you understand how to get at the true issue at hand with a new question. Then I encourage you to bravely attempt to formulate your new question. But first, imagine what you might say to someone else who asked that question, and how you would relate the answer to them, whether it was positive or negative.

For example, a common question to which many people would not like to know the answer is "When and how will I die?" There are many reasons why this question might not be a pleasant one. What if you get the answer wrong? Or, even scarier, what if you get the answer right? That person might become depressed and not enjoy life as much, or live dangerously or even attempt suicide if he or she knew the date of death was fast approaching. If it is wrong, it might cause that person to avoid an activity he or she enjoys, or to make risky choices thinking that they were safe until the appointed time of death. The fundamental question itself may be flawed, since it does not take into account how our choices continually affect our lives and can change our future. After all, that is the entire point of getting psychic readings in the first place.

So, what is the true purpose of that question, anyway, besides simple morbid curiosity? Perhaps the asker is more interested in avoiding an early death. In these cases, one might change the question to, "What should I be primarily thinking about in order to prolong my life as much as possible?" Maybe the person asking wonders if he or she would be able to tie up specific loose ends before leaving the earth. In that case, the person need only ask, "What should be my primary focus as I prioritize my end-of-life planning?" Open questions help guide life actions in a more positive way rather than focusing on a random point in time or specific bad choice that might occur.

Two Truths And A Lie Psychic Game

Here's a way to practice working with someone in person, and at the same time hone your psychic skills with the sense of touch. The following exercise is based on an activity I learned in childhood that is similar to the game "Two Truths and a Lie." In the original activity, my teacher asked each student to bring in an object of special importance to them that had an important life story that went along with it. The object was brought hidden in a paper bag and given to the teacher. She then pulled them out of the bags and set all of them out on a table. Each student was told to pick up and tell a story about three objects, only one of which was theirs and only one of which was true. The rest of the students had to guess which story was real, and which was just a tall tale about somebody else's object.

To play a similar game with a partner to test your own psychic abilities, have a friend or two each come over and bring a few objects. Some should be very meaningful and associated with an important life event, while others should just be everyday objects of no importance. Try holding an object and closing your eyes to wait for perceptions about it. If you are having trouble, you can prompt yourself by meditating and recreating the object through visualization. Some psychics can then visualize more about the object's meaning and a person's experiences with it. Other psychics have extreme experiences where they might feel as if they were the ones using the object during an exceptional event. An ability to be clairtangent is how some psychics solve murder cases by simply touching evidence from the case, as they might have an experience that feels just like being the victim or the perpetrator.

This exercise is especially useful for learning to read for others because messages received can often be very vivid psychic experiences. Capturing the important details in your mind and communicate them clearly afterward can be hard. Practicing this skill is the only way to improve yourself, so dive right in and don't be afraid if at first it feels impossible to explain. Like any life-changing event such as skydiving or giving birth, it might be too emotionally overwhelming to express anything more than "Wow, that was cool" at first. Give yourself time to process and perhaps a few minutes to write down your feelings before trying to express to the person what you experienced.

....

Homework

Solo

Try the exercise in this chapter to ask yourself a difficult question. After you've put a brave foot forward and attempted to use your psychic ability to answer a question surrounding an issue that might feel difficult, you might have a deeper feeling for what it is like for someone who is getting a psychic reading from you. My next homework assignment for you is to go to a professional psychic on your own and have a psychic reading performed for you. Don't take any friends or moral support with you. Instead, bring some equally serious questions as the ones you've already addressed during this homework assignment.

If this will be your first experience receiving a psychic reading, take notes and pay close attention to how you feel during the reading process. How does your mind flow over the material as it is given to you? How do you feel emotionally before, during, and after the reading? Think about how you might maximize the experience for other people who come to you for a psychic reading.

If you're old hat at this and frequently receive psychic readings, go to a new psychic reader. Take notes and pay attention to how he or she chooses to explain things to you. What parts of the reading were too fast or confusing? What parts of the reading might have been slow or boring? How would you have presented the information differently? In what ways did the reading blow you away? What about this psychic reader's technique do you hope to be able to adopt for yourself?

I find it fun to go to other psychic readers on a regular basis. Even if your psychic talents seem to improve on their own, you can always sharpen your method of relating the information you get to others. Sometimes it takes another person's perspective to inspire us to greater improvements.

With a Partner

The object of this chapter is to get you started performing psychic readings for others, so obviously it helps to practice with a partner. You may start with a sympathetic person like a very good friend who will humor you as you look up symbols or tarot card meanings, or speak out loud as you try to figure out what your brain or your spirituality is trying to tell you from the source of your psychic information. However, I firmly believe that it was the frequency of my practice that allowed me to become comfortable with the process and move past the awkwardness of relating to someone else as a psychic.

For that reason, you're going to have to rally more than just one enthusiastic friend and one kooky relative to try out your new skills. Make a commitment, such as performing a reading a day for an entire month, and then look for people to fill those slots. Sure, some people will want more than one reading and that is okay, but space them out so that you can get a variety of experiences and responses.

With the use of the Internet, you may merely have to put out a call for requests on forums related to psychic work to receive a virtual flood of messages from interested people in your email inbox. So determine a pace you can keep up for a sustained period of time. You do need your practice, but it is also quite easy to become burned out on psychic readings if you do too much at once, especially if you are just beginning. Consequently, your feedback regarding how you communicate your readings might sometimes be negative at first.

In order to practice readings frequently, you may have a lot of volunteer subjects that are at a distance from you and psychic readings you perform over the telephone or Internet. However, it is important to hone your in person skills as well, since talking to a person face to face about intimate details of his or her life is very different from an anonymous method of communication that allows you to be more detached or to have less inhibitions. Try playing the "Two Truths and a Lie" psychic game provided in this chapter to practice.

7 Where to Go From Here

So you wanted to be a psychic, and if you've successfully worked with some of the instructions in this book, you are a psychic. So, what do you do next with your newfound powers? You're not likely to be receiving phone calls from talk show hosts just yet. If you believe in fate and destiny, you know that there was a purpose for becoming a psychic. You've learned a lot more about yourself during the process, and now you'll need to find ways to continue growing and using your skills so they don't get rusty.

You can and should establish a regular psychic regimen for solving life's problems. If you slow down and consult your source of psychic information before making big decisions, you'll find yourself making choices that feel right to you more often. Likewise, you can volunteer your psychic services to help other people in need. Psychic readings can be fun gifts for charity fundraisers, or can be bartered for services from others. Who knows, you might even make a name for yourself.

How to Be a Professional

Becoming a professional psychic was a natural step for me as it has for many others once requests for readings started to become so numerous and time-consuming that compensation became mandatory in order to continue devoting quality effort to the craft that is psychic work. Though I started out with psychic readings as a personal spiritual practice and as something I performed for friends and family, I soon branched out. The first time I charged for readings was by offering them during a charity fundraiser for a Pagan student group at my university.

Later I tried my hand at nearly every way to deliver psychic readings. I did them everywhere; at metaphysical bookstores, coffee shops, fairs and carnivals, psychic hotlines, and local parties. I've even given readings on a psychic-themed cruise ship with my mother working alongside me giving readings of her own. I've had experience with the good, the bad, and the ugly with regard to professional psychic work, and I wouldn't have it any other way. However you choose to be a professional psychic, I'd like to show you the way and welcome you to what I think is the very best job on earth.

How to Get Started
As a Professional Psychic

Step 1:
Figure out if you really want to be a professional psychic

Let's start with the job description of a professional psychic. "Psychic" isn't a job you'll see posted on any employment board even though there are companies that do hire psychics. So before you get started as a professional, you'd better know what your job will be. Better yet, you should know what your job will *not* be so you won't waste a lot of time and energy. I'd like to list a few things that a professional psychic is not.

A psychic is not a best friend who says, "Girl, you know that man is bad news! Stay away from him!" While a certain amount of friendly rapport and camaraderie may be what drew you to the field, and the amount of self-disclosure that clients choose to confide in you bolsters that feeling, don't fall into the best friend trap. You will have to hurt your clients sometimes with the news you share and you may have to be firm with them in a way that would seem cold and cruel towards a best friend. So how can you look forward to your next call if it isn't from your best friend? When I was a school teacher, I assumed at first that I would like and enjoy every child. Not every child is a joy to teach, but I found that you can treat people of all ages with respect and serve them well even when you do not love them as a best friend. Not only does keeping professional boundaries keep one safe, it kept me from playing favorites with the children. Likewise, it can keep you from playing favorites with your clients.

A psychic is not a crisis hotline. Imagine your phone is ringing in the middle of the night. You jump out of bed and answer it to find it is a client, crying and distraught. Your husband nods knowingly as you exit the room to your office. He knows you have work to do. While this image might sound romantic to those of us who love to feel needed, it is the quickest route to burnout. No single person is equipped to serve as a crisis hotline. A helper personality can easily be drawn to the excitement of being there for clients at all costs, and I do mean costs. The trouble begins with one sob story about not having the means to pay. If you fancy yourself a crisis hotline, you'll soon be up at all hours of the night giving free readings to those in need. I know, because that was me ten years ago. Set your boundaries now. If people can't afford readings, chances are they know what their priority should be right now without a reading, so you need not let yourself feel bullied into service. You need to help yourself first in order to help others, and serving as the world's crisis hotline might actually be an obstacle standing between your beloved clients and the help they truly need.

A psychic is not a physician. If I had a nickel for every time a woman asked me if she was pregnant...hey wait a minute, if I *charged* a nickel every time, I would be rich. Pregnancy questions may seem ridiculous to you, but it is easier than you think to get sucked into giving advice for that which you are unqualified. It takes valuable time and money away from the client that could be spent on a doctor or a pregnancy test. While divination can be a healthy part of family planning, say it out loud to yourself now, "I am not a doctor!" Now, don't forget to say it out loud to your clients, too.

A psychic is not an attorney. No matter what your per minute or hourly charge, you may still be more affordable than the lawyer the client needs. Strangely enough, the less qualified you are to answer a question, the more you may talk yourself into advising on the matter, thinking there are already procedures in motion or that you are about as unbiased a third party as your client can get. There are free attorneys available for consultation in many areas if the client does some digging, and in criminal cases your client or the subject of his or her reading may already have been appointed one. While you may be an important part of your clients' lives, make sure they've spoken to an attorney first.

A psychic is not a financial planner. More than the previous two cases, this is the area of life in which clients may not even know they have a qualified professional who can provide advice. On top of that, money is often one of the top topics of psychic readings next to love. If you were to allow yourself, you could easily fill your day advising on property values, family assets, divorce allocations, and even stocks. Make sure your clients know there are people out there who actually *do* have this as part of their job descriptions.

By now you are starting to get a pretty good idea of what you will not be when you are a professional psychic. However, you certainly will have a lot of work cut out for you. Just how will you be spending all your time and energy in your new path? Here are a few words that should be on every job description for a professional psychic.

"Counselor." Counseling is providing advice and guidance. In my state, one must be registered as a counselor in order to charge money for such. Becoming a counselor may bring with it other duties you didn't expect. There may be continuing education required, and you may be a "mandated reporter," meaning that legally you must break client confidentiality to report to authorities in cases where clients are a danger to themselves or others, or are gravely disabled. Are you ready to take on those extra obligations?

"Emotional Dumping Ground." I'll admit this phrase was my husband's choice of words, not mine. As a psychic, you are often the only person to whom a client may feel it is socially acceptable to unload negative energy. If you don't have shields, whether they be metaphorical or metaphysical, you'll quickly be burned out of the business. Emotional dumping can be unintentional, such as simply causing pain in an empath when a client chooses to unburden his or her life story. Or the dumping can be direct in the form of angry phone calls or vicious ratings left after a reading. If you are not prepared to deal with the incredible influx of emotional energy that can come from clients and even other readers, please give serious consideration to how deeply you wish to involve yourself with this line of work.

"Business Owner." If you're working in person in many contexts, you'll need to get a license for your business in your state and possibly your city. Being a business owner is a full-time job in and of itself. You may have to scout brick-and-mortar locations for your business, hire employees or contractors, and find out all of the legal nuances of working in your area. If this seems like too much work that is not directly involved with your true calling, consider working for a company and scrapping the idea of starting up your own website or store before it snowballs into something too tiring and costly.

"Accountant." You owe federal and possibly state taxes, potentially paid quarterly. You'll have to account for every transaction, with receipts when necessary, and make note of any write-offs. Even if you hire your own accountant, there's a lot of work that must be done directly by you if you are working in multiple contexts. Again, if this is something so far away from your true calling that you wish to avoid it like the plague, I suggest choosing a company for which to work and making sure they are legitimate and competent enough to account for your earnings themselves.

"Marketer." So you've done all the work of setting up your own website or shop or signing up with a company you like. Why isn't your phone ringing off the hook yet? The psychic industry is enormous and in constant flux with tremendous numbers of talented competitors. Even if you are incredibly skilled and confident that word of mouth will spread, up until this point of your life that same word of mouth has only gotten you to where you are at this moment. Unless you promote yourself—up to and including paying for advertising—you may find yourself frustrated by a lack of clients or by low call volume.

Step 2:
Choose how you want to work

If you're still reading this after learning the true job description of the professional psychic, perhaps it really is your calling. The first decision that you'll have to make is whether to start off working as a psychic for an existing company, or whether to go into business for yourself right away. Yes, there are companies that need psychics, but I'm afraid that it won't be something exciting like the police force. Instead, your first contract job may likely be with a psychic hotline.

"Thank you for calling the psychic network, my identification number is..." For some, it is a matter of pride. For others, it is appalling. Years after the public fiasco with "Miss Cleo" and the Psychic Reader's Network which put hotlines in a bad light, some of these companies have continued to work hard to be ethical. They screen their lines appropriately for clients that might otherwise give you a hard time and some even send you a gift for the holidays.

Companies usually value their readers' privacy, allowing you to work under an alias without clients knowing your phone number, contact information, or anything about you. After all, if you go into business on your own, you become a public figure of sorts, since oftentimes your face and name will be tied to the real you, especially when doing in-person readings. Companies also work on advertising, though you may still have to do some of your own. Working for a company either online or on the telephone might mean that you don't have to worry about processing the money or pricing, with some companies even offering direct deposit. Working for a company can be easier and it may feel more secure to be receiving a regular paycheck from a job. It can be very rewarding, as many companies offer special bonuses for working longer hours or for other exemplary service. Some telephone lines or online companies can pair you with a mentor or introduce you to a community of psychics who can help you improve your work.

I'll admit that I might be pushing the idea of working for a company but that is because I truly believe that this is the best way for a beginning professional psychic to jump into the business. When first starting out, working for a company can outshine self-employment, since it is hard to combine both learning the psychic trade with learning how to own your own business. After all, owning your own business means bootstrapping yourself. You do all your own advertising, and you screen all of your clients—from the good to the very bad. You would have to get yourself a business license and comply with all your regional laws. You'd have to track all of your earnings and pay annual, and in some cases quarterly, taxes. When you work for yourself, you're a part-time psychic and a full-time business owner. If all of that would distract from what you truly want to do, then it is time to just get yourself a contract job.

Your first step is to pick the right company. There are many out there, and they all have different pay rates and policies. You might do well to speak with another professional psychic in your area to ask him or her for a review of companies he or she has tried. Working for one company for a while and then quitting is okay, but I have found through my own experiences that if you want to make a career out of working for a company, it is best not to work for more than one at a time. Splitting up your working hours would mean the company's clients couldn't come to depend on your availability, which would lead to being unable to build a client base that can sustain a livable wage.

How to Write a
Professional Code of Ethics

American pacifist and 1931 Nobel Peace Prize winner Jane Addams once said, "Action indeed is the sole medium of expression for ethics." As psychics who read for other people, we are thrust or driven to the position of spiritual leaders. Whether or not we openly accept responsibility for this role, this sacred trust has already been gifted to us by our clients. While we may all be adept at communicating our ethics and morals, they are all without value if we do not live them.

All of us live to our own standards of right and wrong, but those standards might blur or shift depending on circumstance. Thinking of yourself as standing firmly by your ethics is easy. You may decide that you would never try to help somebody in a manner beyond your expertise, but if a client is standing there with a large wad of money in hand, you may decide that perhaps the reason you've never been able to help such a person before is because you've never tried.

In order to truly take a measure of your current ethical standing, I encourage every psychic to write his or her own personal code of ethics. That way, if you do choose to reevaluate your ethical life, you can do so with accuracy. There are several circumstances which arouse ethical considerations in those with a shared morality that you may consider addressing in your personal code.

The match of your own personal belief system with that of the person for whom you are reading can be an important consideration to many clients of yours. For example, some people may have strong Christian beliefs that can make it difficult for them to approach psychics due to passages in the Bible which prohibit divination and spiritualism. For such reasons, they may seek out angel readers or advice without divination. Even if you don't fit into that category, it can be easy to put on a happy face and pretend that you are something you are not simply because you don't believe in those Bible verses. However not only are you unknowingly putting the client in what he or she might consider spiritual jeopardy, you're starting off your relationship with the client on the wrong foot by not being totally honest about your belief system. Sprinkle a little of the belief system that informs your readings throughout your written personal code of ethics.

The age of the clients you serve can be called into question for multiple reasons. First of all, since minors cannot legally enter into contracts themselves, from a purely legal standpoint in your area you may not be permitted to read for children, nor would they be able to make agreements about your terms of service on their own. While some readers will gladly read for children with a parent or guardian present, others believe that some forms of wisdom may not be appropriate for those under the age of eighteen, twenty-one, until after his or her astrological Saturn return, or even under age forty. Make your own decisions now before a child at a fair is waving cash under your nose asking for a reading.

Many clients value confidentiality, and it is an important consideration even if you have already decided to not sell anyone's name or contact information and not share identifying information in publications or in your autobiography. Begin with those obvious points, and decide now whether you'd sell a list of email addresses for a lot of money, or whether you'd like to end your career with a dazzling, tell-all book about the celebrities for whom you have read. Afterwards, consider some more mundane situations. What would you do if a husband and wife each came to you for readings on their marriage, unbeknownst to each other? Would you be biased if you knew the husband was cheating? Would you share the truth of what you knew with the wife if you knew it would influence her decisions? Conundrums with client confidentially can and do happen. What would you do if a client you knew well threatened suicide or even murder? What if a client was refusing to go to the hospital for a critical illness? Under what circumstances would you share client information? Make this clear in your personal code of ethics.

Nearly all honest readers begin their careers believing that they will always share the truth with their clients, no matter what. But this self-policing is often what first falls to the wayside. Consider a situation where a fifteen-year-old girl at a birthday party asks whether her dad's smoking is going to kill him and you do see death by lung cancer in his future. Do you tell the child? Do you lie, or do you back out of the reading completely? That situation may be rare, but it does happen—it happened to me. A more common situation is on a website or a telephone network on which there are ratings, when a client comes to you and makes it quite clear he or she wants to hear good news. If you tell him or her bad news, you receive a very negative rating. After a few of those slaps to the face, readers are often tempted to paint a rosy future in order to receive the rewards of positive ratings and even large financial tips and bonuses. Make an agreement with yourself now about where you stand with honesty, and what you will do when your boundaries are pushed. Write this in your personal code of ethics.

While you're on an honesty kick, decide now which types of people in this world you can and cannot read. Acknowledging your prejudices may be beneficial, but it can be even more difficult for a client to run into a judgmental reader. Can you honestly advise a woman having an affair if you are biased towards monogamy? Do you welcome gay and lesbian clients? Are you a pet psychic, or do you believe that animals do not have souls? Be up front with the client base you wish to support, otherwise you will be giving poor service to a client base you don't even want.

I have already stated that psychics are not qualified to give financial advice unless they are qualified financial advisors and not qualified to give legal advice unless they are attorneys. Of course psychics can be used to supplement the advice of other professionals, and in the hustle and bustle of online competition for psychic work, it can be easy to make harmful assumptions about whom the client has already consulted. No matter how many times a day you read or hear the question, "Am I pregnant?" decide now what your first reaction shall be every time. Include a list of local, national, and international hotlines, and free referral services for problems with suicide, rape, physical abuse, shelter, substance abuse, family planning, and anything else you find coming your way.

The most dangerous ethical state of mind for a good psychic is complacency. Deciding that you will never be tempted to change your ethical position or to step outside of your own ethical boundaries is an easy pitfall. For example, many married couples are certain that they will never find anyone outside the marriage attractive, and are astounded when something "just happens" with another person outside the marriage, deciding that it was proof the marriage wasn't right in the first place. However, couples who acknowledge outside attractions and take intentional actions not to put themselves in positions that risk their values are less likely to commit infidelity. Likewise, if you acknowledge that you are human and may someday be tempted do something outside of your ethics whether it be for a large sum of money or for a client who just seems so desperate that you want to help at all costs, you will be prepared for when that can and does happen.

Begin by writing out that code of ethics and deciding what you will do in each case if you are pushed. For each situation, find yourself an appropriate referral, as that will help you to end the temptation quickly and assist the client. At a fair, you might pick out a booth suitable for children if you have decided not to read for them, and direct the children there. If you don't believe in angels, find an angel reader you respect to whom you can send business. Most importantly, allow yourself to honestly reevaluate your personal code of ethics on a regular basis, such as on your birthday or New Year's Day. Change your written ethics if they no longer match how you have grown as a person. Be especially vigilant for things that you should add to your code of ethics that you may not have yet encountered at the time you originally wrote it. Your code will be a living document, just as your ethics should be expressed throughout your changing life.

Step 3:
Get a job

Once you've chosen a company for which you want to make a good effort to work, the next step after application will most likely be a test reading. Think of this as your job interview. For a new psychic, this might feel quite nerve-wracking, indeed. The first things you should be prepared for are questions regarding your background and experience. My tip for you is to remember who you are talking with here. You might be accustomed to taking such questions from people who want a reading from you by answering with a long explanation designed to help a friend or relative understand how a psychic comes to be. Your interviewer is familiar with psychics already and doesn't want to hear your life's story. Rather, he or she is probing to understand what belief systems inform your readings and in what contexts you've already gained a comfortable rapport with clients doing readings.

The question about your beliefs is the first point in your interview where your honesty will be tested, so do not let yourself down. For example, if you believe that the tarot cards are merely a psychological tool representing Jungian archetypes, now is not the time to weave an elaborate lie about how you talk to angels or were initiated into witchcraft and magically receive messages from the divine. Likewise, if you hear voices from gods, it is important not to dumb down your beliefs and just say you're a simple astrologer. Believing that you are a psychic to a "crazy" degree, or not believing that you are "psychic" at all in the traditional sense, will not immediately ruin your chances as an employee. Also, be aware that your interviewer may be helping the company build your profile, and it is important that you don't start a snowball of dishonesty that ends up in some poor client's lap.

The second part of the interview process may be the most anxiety inducing; the test reading. Your interviewer will begin by requesting a general reading for you. The key here is to start in the way that best showcases your strengths. If you use a divinatory system, start your reading in a way that requires the least information from the other person. For example, astrology or numerology might not be the best way to start, since asking a series of even reasonable questions might make you seem like you're stalling, at best; or cold reading, at worst. If you have a number of other choices of ways to read, begin in the way you are the most comfortable and fluid. Your first choice may be a reading style or divination tool with which you have the most experience. Then, push yourself by moving on to another style or tool that may be unique or rare to your interviewer, even if you are less skilled with it. Your interviewer is looking for somebody who is relaxed and comfortable reading, but also somebody who might draw additional clients to their line or keep clients coming back for more. So, for example, if you are very comfortable with tarot cards, you can begin with a tarot reading to showcase your experience, and then shift at a natural point into a rune casting to highlight your growth and diversity as a reader.

After you've blown them away with your reading, don't be afraid to ask questions about the company. Take notes as you ask what pay rate they will offer you to start and the maximum pay you can expect to receive. Press to find out if you are expected to collect client information or perform any other job function besides reading. Find out the time commitment required. They know that as a skilled and talented reader you have a wide range of choices as to which company to choose, so make them work to convince you that they are the right company for the job.

Once you've chosen a company, commit yourself to as many hours as you possibly can maintain. At first, if you have flexibility, try all hours of the day. If you are working phone lines, you may find that the nighttime and weekend hours are most busy. Or, if it is an international company, you might find a sudden influx of calls when another country wakes up for their day, or gets home from work. As soon as you've tried out a week of this, set more firm and predictable hours, so that your clients can get to know when they can reach you and rely on your help.

Start to promote your shifts and yourself when you can. Make yourself some business cards and take pride in your work. Ask your company how to market yourself—they will readily have suggestions for you. Learning about promotion can be good practice if you want to later on start a business of your own. Be aware that you'll have to start from scratch getting new clients, as most companies have firm policies against stealing clients—and they are happy to enforce this with legal action.

Once you've spent a number of years working as a contract psychic, I suspect you will want to go into business for yourself. Some companies might even cause you to rebel against working for them as time goes on. Though less common in this day in age, there was a time when almost all hotlines had a strict quota of average minutes for you to reach, which still happens in some cases. One company for which I've worked even pushed their readers to ask each client to take a customer survey while the client's money was being eaten up during the time in which they should have been getting a reading.

No matter how well the company for which you work matches up to your core values, you'll be working for the company's best interest, not your own. The same things that protect you when you're working in a company also limit you. Most companies don't allow you to give out your own contact information or any "off-site" information. So if you're hoping to promote yourself or to recommend a book or a website, you cannot. Most companies don't allow you to set your own price, which can be very limiting. For example, the industry average here in the United States is currently about $0.30 per minute at the time of this writing. That may seem to be fair, amounting to $18 an hour, at first. But, realistically, you won't be talking every minute of every hour of your work day. Also, when you remove at least a third of that for taxes, your maximum potential earnings might be less than minimum wage in your state.

Step 4:
Work independently

In my experience, good professionals who decide that psychic work feels right to them eventually choose to start being more independent. When working for yourself, not only do you have unlimited earning potential, but your activities are unlimited. You can become close, personal friends with your clients. You can set your own prices and raise or lower them at will. When I want to do telephone or email or chat readings all day long, I can. When I want to read at a city fair or even on a cruise ship in the Bahamas, I can. You can't suffer burnout unless you burn your own self out.

In order to start your own psychic business, you must first make yourself aware of regional laws as they relate to business ownership as well as psychic work. In some areas, fortune-telling is either illegal or highly regulated. As mentioned earlier, for example, my state requires credentials given by the department of health in order to be in any situation where you give personal advice. Requiring credentials is in order to have an organized complaint system for people who abuse their authority when behind closed doors. And I support it. As a result, psychics around me are getting their Certified Advisor credential or similar. I myself currently hold a Certified Counselor credential, for which I was required to take classes as well as pass an examination and find a supervisor. Becoming a counselor may seem impractical, but it is the only way to legally be a psychic in many areas, and is a good idea in all cases.

Before I began charging money for giving advice, I also had to get a business license. You will need a license for every area in which you do business. So, if you have an office in two cities within one state, you might need a state business license as well as a business license for each of the cities in which you work. Hire yourself an accountant, as there may also be federal, state, and city taxes that apply to the ways you do business. Taxes may change as your business model changes. After all, you'll have to decide where you'll be working.

You might choose to only work from home, via your telephone or the internet, and pay for a bank's merchant services to manage your payments. However, if you want to meet with people in person, you would do well to experiment with formats before you run out and get yourself entangled in a property purchase or tied down with an expensive leasing situation. The service business model allows us the luxury of operating in different locations, so take advantage of that while you learn your own personal preferences.

Step 5:
Gather and maintain a portion of in-person clientele

In my opinion, the best way to start out with in-person readings is at fairs and festivals. Festival environments allow you to be exposed to many people and you can see if you're cut out for long hours and strange characters. Look for local seasonal festivals as well as psychic fairs and mind and body expos. You may need to buy a few chairs and a tent-style booth and then pay a fee for the privilege of using the space. Though I no longer do fairs since it is not the best use of my time and money, I don't regret the years I spent traveling to various events. Events allowed me to learn what sorts of clients I liked best, and to start becoming known within my community. Along the way I learned that I really liked working with people in person and that I could handle many clients a day.

If you find that you love working in person but are growing out of the part of your career where you haul a tent around in your car, you can start looking into the idea of having your own space for doing business. It pays to be cautious, however, as this might also be the time that marketing becomes mandatory. After all, you won't have tens of thousands of fairgoers walking past your front door anymore. See if you can market yourself enough to make a living by first forming a partnership with a local business.

Pound the pavement and visit some potential business partners. Look into local bookstores, coffee shops, and wellness centers. Investigate anywhere that might have a table and chairs for you, event space for you to host parties, or even an office space. I've worked in partnership with a candle shop and a bar, but metaphysical bookstores are usually the most friendly to this sort of arrangement. Offer to pay to use some space in which to conduct your business. I find that the best arrangement is to offer a percentage of your earnings, rather than a flat fee, since you might not be able to immediately obtain a steady stream of clients.

Step 6:
Promote yourself and network with other psychics
Finally, you'll have to begin advertising. Unfortunately there's no magic recipe for that, since it requires plenty of trial and error to find your own marketing plan. Even then it will change from season to season and year to year as your business grows and changes. All I can advise is that you not be afraid to invest in yourself by paying for advertising, though be sure to keep meticulous records so you can figure out what is working and more deserving of your attention and what isn't, requiring brainstorming some new angles.

Now that you've started on your lifelong career path, reach deeper into your community and make friends with the other local professional psychics who are now your colleagues. See each other not just as faceless competition.

After all, you can refer business to each other. I often send clients to other local psychics I know are good people if I have a conflicting appointment. In turn, I sometimes hit a bonanza when another psychic retires and sends his or her entire client base my way.

There are no substitutes to take your place when you're sick, just like there are no automatic health insurance or retirement plans unless you work on making your own. Plan ahead as you enjoy your new responsibilities for yourself and your clients. After all, you are the psychic. Thinking about the future should be one of the things you do best.

How to Retire as a Professional Psychic

You'll need to find another psychic you trust so that you can plan for the end of your psychic reading days. If you've always wanted to be a psychic, now that you are one, it is never too early to begin planning for your retirement. I don't just mean investing in an Individual Retirement Account. After all, if you do choose to read for others, whether for money or not, there may come a time when you wish to focus on other things in your life.

Even if in your excitement you can't imagine ever stopping being the friendly neighborhood psychic, make a backup plan anyway to create a glowing memory of your career. Intuitive spiritual leaders don't necessarily lead a charmed and changeless life. After all, what psychic wants to have to hang up a sign that says "Closed Forever Due to Unforeseen Circumstances" and then hear everyone laugh and say, "Shouldn't she have seen it coming?" Eventually, your own destiny may lead you elsewhere and your career may come to a conclusion after giving to you everything it was meant to give you. Retirement and moving on to new phases of life are neither shocking nor unusual, even for psychics. Look forward to the day when you can arrange a grand send-off and allow your community to congratulate you. Retiring is where passing the torch well comes into play.

You don't have the time to personally test each and every psychic you know. Think about the top two roles that your successor must assume. First, he or she must be an example of stability, so look for somebody with longevity in the industry. If your successor happens to go out of business soon after you, it may devastate the people who relied on you. Secondly, he or she should be well connected with a network within the psychic community. Even if you pick the best psychic you've ever experienced, chances are he or she won't be right for everyone. Thus, your successor should also be someone who can continue the referral process and help your clients find the right fit for them long after all of this is far from your mind.

Don't just pick a successor, but work with him or her throughout the process and make sure you're pointing all your signs, phone messages, websites, social networks, and email auto-replies in the right direction. If you're retiring from a psychic business, make sure you report to your federal and state departments of revenue when your business closes. If not, you will still be responsible for filing even if you aren't making a penny. Talk with a financial planner. Are you planning on selling your company? What will happen to your good name and trademarks after you're not watching them like a hawk? Talk with an attorney.

Follow these three tips to tie up loose ends so when you're through being a psychic for other people, you'll have gone a long way towards ensuring that you won't leave gossip and chaos behind you. The only thing to worry about now is stepping forward through that open door to the rest of your experiences. The chapter in your life that was being a psychic is now being written, but the book will be unfinished no matter how long you choose to be a psychic, so don't let it gather dust under the bed. Whether you will give the psychic community decades of steady service, or if this will just be a whirlwind adventure for you, I wish you and yours luck in whatever new destiny you've chosen.

Ghost Hunting

Aside from the professional psychic, the other face of the psychic in popular culture today is the ghost hunter, as made popular by countless reality television show episodes. I grew up when the *Ghostbusters* movies were popular, so there's nobody out there who would love to make a living doing that more than me, though I admit that ghost hunting today is a hobby and not a career. Though I have received the occasional unsolicited donation after performing an exorcism or a banishing for someone in need, there simply isn't enough demand out there to warrant a well-compensated service provider.

In my belief, ghosts are more common than many people might realize. Since I tend to see and hear them, I find them to be quite common in populated areas. However, I believe that they are usually more like natural paranormal fauna, rather than an infestation that needs to be managed. So, unless there's extenuating circumstances such as murder, suicide, or some other unusual malice, I've found there are very few clients who want anything done about a ghost.

That isn't to say that ghosts aren't fascinating and that ghost hunting isn't a worthwhile hobby, I just wouldn't flatter myself by attempting to make it into a money-making venture. Instead, join a local paranormal group, or grab a few adventurous friends, and have fun investigating the weird and wonderful world of the unknown after death.

In order to hunt a ghost, you may not even have to go further than your own home. As I said, I find that ghosts are more common in populated areas than most people realize. I think it is funny when people ask me if there are any local old "haunted houses." Are there many old buildings on which previous occupants haven't left their spiritual mark, I wonder? If you believe that having a death occur in a home increases the chance of a haunting, pay close attention next time you visit a large and busy hospital—deaths happen there all the time. In my beliefs, I find that hospitals are, in fact, filled with many ghosts. But you might make a nuisance of yourself if you make that your reason for visiting one.

Before you scout out a location for your ghost hunting, stay home and practice your psychic skills with the dead. Mediumship sittings, dumb suppers, and practicing with your six senses and your divination skills can help you become more immediately aware of a supernatural presence before you go out into the wild to hunt one down. Once you decide to go on a field trip, however, make sure that you get the permission of those who own or manage the property before you start snooping around.

The best places to take your group of ghost enthusiasts are places of historical importance. If you call ahead of time to let the staff know about your purpose, you may be greeted with excitement. History buffs often think it would be rather neat if you were able to have a deeper connection with the subjects of their study, and many volunteer to allow you greater access or to give you a guided tour of a location. Having a historian with your group can be a wonderful way to verify your psychic information immediately, and to clear up any confusing messages you receive.

For example, a historical site local to me, Meeker Mansion in Kent, Washington, is extremely friendly and open to psychics. So much so that psychic fairs are hosted there for the public to come and enjoy. A historical society has been working to restore the mansion to 1891 conditions, when it was completed and occupied by the Meeker couple,

Ezra and Eliza Jane. The house is a veritable museum of vintage artifacts from the Meeker family.

I can't tell you how fun it was to investigate the house with a bunch of fellow psychics. Many of my colleagues rushed upstairs, drawn by a mysterious feeling of energy. I recall that I saw many ghosts, and asked "why are there so many old people here?" I was told that the mansion had later been turned into a nursing home, which explained to me why I saw so many ghosts that did not seem to be associated with the Meeker family and their time. Discovering surprising new pieces of information can be fun and educational for yourself, even if you're not helping anyone in particular or making money.

Another example of working with fun history buffs was when I connected with a ghost of a person who once lived on some specific property. I sent an email to the historical society associated with the area with the name the ghost gave, along with her year of birth and a few details about her, such as what instrument she played in the school band, and her manner of death. Even though I sent out the email quite late in the evening, a historian replied at two in the morning, so great was his excitement. He sent me a photograph of her when she was living, and pointed me to some newspaper articles from that time that confirmed the other details. So, even though I didn't really solve a problem this time with my psychic work, I sure made someone's day.

Another purpose of psychic work I should address is the number of psychic shows on television (at the time of this writing). I must assume that some of you want to be a psychic so you can be famous. However, the rising popularity means that there are plenty of potentials in an already-competitive field. Being a good psychic isn't an automatic golden ticket into the entertainment business.

If being a television psychic is your eventual goal, I suggest you get started like any other entertainment hopeful. Make sure you are well-rounded and schooled in the other skills television producers will want you to have. Take voice and diction classes, or join an improvisational group. Sign up to work as an extra on movie, television, or commercial sets, and make connections with people in the industry. Network with casting directors for reality television and talk with your local talent agencies that represent people who do unscripted work. Understand that you may have to work for free for those who are taping pilot episodes, and know that the entertainment industry is feast or famine.

You may not be able to sustain a livable wage while you work to hit the big time, but it could offer opportunities to advertise yourself if you also run your own psychic business. So, put on your best face, and work hard to represent yourself well as a psychic so that you promote our work as a whole. Every public psychic is an ambassador for the rest of the world's psychics, so please take that responsibility seriously.

How to Deal with
Ridicule and Naysayers

No matter how wonderful a psychic you are, you will be met with opposition from others if you are public about it. There are many people who believe that psychics are crazy at best and evil at worst. Even if you come from the school of thought that bullies are to be ignored, this can often be impossible. For example, if you are a professional psychic and the negativity is coming from a client, you must be able to handle the situation maturely. Consider the scenario below.

As soon as Alicia picked up the phone, she knew that this was not going to be a good call. She was a psychic, after all. Almost right off the bat, the client was combative. When Alicia asked him what questions he would like answered, he shot back that she should know since she was a psychic and interjected that he already thought she was a fake. She was hurt to her core. After all, this was her true calling in life. As the telephone conversation progressed, it became more abusive, degenerating into a session of name-calling. The client was yelling at the top of his lungs and slammed the phone down.

Alicia was physically shaken after the call. She could feel her hands trembling and her heart pounding. She knew she could give no more good readings at the moment. She immediately stopped taking calls in order to recover from the experience. Her initial subjective experience wasn't the end of her ordeal. Her angry client was able to leave a rating for her through the internet site on which she was working, and she knew the rating wouldn't be good. Alicia stayed logged out from the telephone lines and website the rest of the day. The next day, not only did she not want to be victimized again, she knew her bad rating would drive away clients. Again, she took a day off of work. By the end of the week, she had given up her dream job.

The above story may be a bit exaggerated, but it is not unheard of, and elements of it are recognizable to all experienced psychics. To new psychics, I am proud to say that most of the clients in our industry are absolute treats to work with. However, since burnout is the number one reason I've seen psychics leave the business, it does not behoove new psychics to pretend that a negative experience with a client will never happen. I will examine how to deal with a negative client before, during, and after the encounter, so that not only will the experience not turn you off from the best job in the world, but perhaps the experience will help you become a better psychic. I've used the acronym AUM, the universal sound of peace, to help you remember to stay calm and use the encounter for your own personal gain throughout the experience. AUM stands for Avoidance, Understanding, and Meditation.

Before: Avoidance
Of course, the ultimate avoidance is to not give readings at all, so I'd like to briefly acknowledge that being a professional psychic is not a job for everyone, especially on the

telephone or internet. Performing readings in person has the least incidence of negative client interactions in my experience but it is not entirely without them either. When you begin to give readings by telephone or on the Internet—especially through a network that does not screen clients—you will open yourself up to a whole new world of people, good and bad. Choose carefully whether this is a line of work you can both handle and enjoy handling.

Many psychics choose only to work with clients in person, but if you decide you're up for the challenge of telephone or online work, the first thing you should do when writing your profile is include any types of readings you do not perform. If you don't believe in angels, are not a medical intuitive, and cannot find lost objects or give exact time frames, state this openly in your biography and save yourself and clients a lot of heartache. New people: raise your prices. New psychics often undercut other psychics just slightly so they have an edge in call volume. However, there are those out there in the world who find it amusing or fulfilling in some way to hire a low-priced psychic just to give a bad rating or be aggressive during the call. If you raise your price to a respectable amount befitting a professional, you will find more clients who are serious about having a positive reading experience with you.

During: Understanding

Remain professional at all times! Do not resort to name-calling, sarcasm, or a raised voice. As soon as you know you are unable to help a client either before or after you are hired, be honest and let the client know so he or she can end the session early. For example, if the client repeatedly insists he or she wants good news and you aren't seeing it, then let him or her know you don't feel you'll be able to give a positive reading experience. If the client does not choose to end the session and continues to berate you, attempt to turn it into an information gathering session for yourself.

Allow the client to vent, as this may be the purpose that drove the client to call in the first place. Indeed, I have sometimes earned high ratings from angry clients simply by keeping a cool head and accepting any responsibility I could. Apologize for the reading experience not being positive, as that was truly not your intent, and ask the client how he or she might suggest you improve yourself as a reader. If you have the ability, you can offer to refund the client his or her money or ask how you can make it right, although I advise against posting a refund policy openly as that may attract less than honest people who never intend on paying for a reading.

If you work for a company that has a rating system, don't mention it during the session to try to get out of a negative rating. Understand that if you choose to work with such a system, part of your job description is going to be that you are a "punching bag" for ratings. As mentioned before, there are people out there who purchase readings just to give bad ratings, and you are satisfying that need by simply working within that system. If you cannot handle that, it is important to be honest with yourself when choosing which systems under which you will and will not work, so go back to the avoidance stage if you find yourself continuously bringing up ratings with your employer.

After: Meditation

The meditation part is not just going back to the "avoidance" stage and beginning again. Though I recognize you may need some downtime after such a conflict, it is important to make this stage constructive rather than destructive to your career goals. As soon as possible after the encounter and in a confidential way, take notes on what happened. Include contributing factors leading up to the event and quote comments the client made. In fact, you may wish to begin this practice with exceptionally good calls too, so you can observe your strengths and weaknesses more accurately. If you work for a company, notify your superior about what happened so that you can gain extra assistance from a mentor if available and so that the client can be noted in case a pattern of reader abuse develops. Next, settle down and reflect on how you can improve as a reader. Even if the feedback from the client is outrageously untrue, there may be hidden nuggets of truth or there may have been ways you were unconsciously encouraging those incorrect perceptions. Is there anything you could have done to avoid or understand that client more effectively? Brainstorm and write down wild guesses as to what you can do differently. Make sure that you write

SMART goals—Specific, Measurable, Attainable, Realistic, and Timely—for next time.

Yes, there *will* be a "next time" because what comes after this is the hardest part. As soon as possible after you have recovered from the encounter, make yourself available and take on a new client. In your very next session, put at least one of your new goals into practice. Even if this isn't the best reading of your career, the aim is to make it more positive than your last.

The good thing about being a professional psychic is that you are often a lone wolf on your own without anyone looking over your shoulder, judging you. The bad thing about being a professional psychic is that you are often alone without anyone sitting by your side and helping you. Ratings are a poor substitute for personal accountability, so just as you might think that running screaming for the hills is a bad reaction to a difficult client, simply shrugging off the negative reading experience is much worse. There is a dearth of professional standards within the psychic industry, which may be part of the problem with a growing group of unsatisfied clients who become difficult during a session. If you've been victimized by a difficult client, you may have unwittingly become part of the problem. Each of us should take intentional steps to become part of the solution with a grassroots effort towards improvement as individuals and as an industry.

Even if you choose to never become a professional psychic, the AUM technique described above can turn any negative reading experience with another person into a way to improve yourself as a psychic. Even if your critic isn't paying you, it does you no good to tune out feedback. Search carefully for the nugget of truth in any critique, and if you can't find one, think about how conveying the message could have been done better. There's always room for improvement.

What if your meanest critics haven't even tried a psychic reading from you? In this case, ignoring such people may be the key to your mental survival. However, there may be several situations in which you might be tempted to face doubt or criticism head-on. For example, if you are simply so overjoyed with your psychic experiences that you want to share it with the world, it is understandable that you might feel the urge to get a little pushy when a friend or acquaintance refuses to even try a psychic reading. You may even feel a little bit insulted. Remember that psychic beliefs are not a gospel that has to be spread. Even if you want to share the joy of your discovery in the same way you might not want to be alone when viewing the most beautiful sunset, respect the beliefs of others just as you would want your beliefs respected whenever it is practical. Form friendships with other psychics and their fans in your area if you would like more support.

Another problem could be that you have family that has a negative attitude toward psychics for whatever reason. If you're a grown person who only sees such family members on the holidays, it might be best to keep your psychic interests to yourself. But if you're tired of trying to hide your beliefs, or if you're a person whose parents disagree with your psychic practice, it is important to learn to resolve your differences or agree to disagree as peacefully as possible.

If a family member tends to think that you are crazy for what you practice, and loudly bemoans how he or she can't understand how such a smart person can believe in psychics, try not to feel frustrated at this insult to your intelligence. Point out that doubt is a good thing and that you are a working hypothesis in progress. After all, you are only doing it because it is fun and it works. Otherwise, there wouldn't be much of a point. Besides, what you are doing makes you happy and doesn't harm anyone.

On the other hand, if a family member has religious beliefs that lead him or her to think that psychics are evil, tread carefully. Think about how brave the family member must be to bring up such a troubling topic, and thank him or her for caring so much about your spiritual well-being. Then, simply state that you have chosen your own course of action and that nothing he or she can say or do will change your mind. Being firm with a sense of finality while remaining sensitive to the beliefs of others can help you preserve friendships and relationships wherever possible.

If the reason you can't ignore the naysayers is because they are part of a governing body that is restricting the free speech and activities of psychics (professional or otherwise), it may be time to fight back. Gather supporters, whether they be colleagues, clients, fans, sympathizers, or groups of similarly ostracized people. Address each and every concern that lead the powers that be to consider banning psychics from any area or practice.

Chances are that the authorities aren't coming down on psychics because they have a bone to pick with you personally. They probably have valid concerns about protecting consumers from crooked psychics, or people masquerading as psychics. But for the same reason that some dishonest mechanics or salesmen haven't caused all of them to be run off the planet, you can help to make sure that a few bad apples won't spoil the psychic bunch.

Think of practical ways to regulate psychics in your area in a manner that protects consumers without making psychic readings impossible. In some cases, this might already have been done for you. In that situation, you may only need to point out that police can enforce existing laws pertaining to theft or fraud committed by psychics or imposters, and that at least in the case of the United States, the Federal Trade Commission takes complaints of false advertising and can bring charges against them.

Of course, we psychics should police ourselves and each other as well. Bad psychics who work for companies can be reported to their superiors and bad companies that work in many states might have reason to be brought to the attention of the Better Business Bureau, the Postmaster General, the Federal Bureau of Investigation, and others. Don't get in a petty personal spat with your neighborhood competitor but don't turn a blind eye to a situation in which a supposed psychic is hurting his or her clients either. As always, be an upstanding example of a psychic yourself, holding yourself to your highest ethical standards.

....

Homework

Solo

Write your own personal code of ethics now, using the instructions in this chapter. Mark your calendar with a review date so you can look over what you've written again. For example, New Year's Day might be a wonderful time to go over your ethics and reflect on any additions or other changes. What better way to start the new year than by improving upon your own ethical standards for the future?

With a Partner

Here is the last homework assignment of the book. If you've been a good new psychic, you've been working on all the homework assignments along the way. Now it is time to branch out and connect with other inspiring people and materials so you won't be stuck navel-gazing at your first efforts for the rest of your psychic career. Join professional or hobby organizations that pertain to divination practices or paranormal investigation activities you enjoy.

Most importantly, find a real live psychic role model you can emulate. I firmly believe in the apprenticeship style of learning for such an individual process as becoming a psychic. Just as I was encouraged to grow by my family and spiritual community, I hope that you too will find at least one supportive mentor.

Now that you've made a connection with one or more psychic mentors of the generation of psychics before you, I hope that you will reach out to pass the light onto those who want to be a psychic after being inspired by your own success. Perhaps someday the person you encouraged to want to be a psychic will take over your business for you when you retire. Share this book with somebody who shows promise as a psychic, and make our community a little brighter.

Glossary

Akashic records: A compilation of mystical knowledge, access to which is sometimes believed to make one omniscient, located on the astral plane.

Astral: A spiritual plane of existence, like a parallel dimension to our own physical plane.

Astral travel: Meditative trance journeying to the astral realm in your mind's eye.

Astrology: A system of divination that uses the arrangements and relative movements of celestial bodies for interpretation.

Aura: A halo of colored light seen by clairvoyants which surrounds people (and sometimes other living or non-living things). An aura is often believed to be associated with energy.

Automatic writing: A form of channeling that allows a source of psychic information to use the psychic medium's hands to write a message.

Channeling: The act of being the direct conduit for communications from a supernatural source.

Chi: Metaphorical or spiritual "energy," the flow of which you can direct with your will in order to manifest things in your life.

Clairaudient: "Clear hearing." Having the ability to receive true messages from a supernatural source in the form of sounds.

Clairsentient: "Clear feeling." Sometimes used in literature to indicate receiving true messages through the perception of touch, but also used a little more figuratively sometimes to include "feeling" emotions.

Clairvoyant: "Clear seeing." Having the ability to receive true messages from a supernatural source in the form of pictures.

Crystal ball: A usually translucent sphere often made of quartz crystal into which one gazes for scrying purposes.

Divination: A system developed with tools in order to look for signs and symbolic meaning through chance arrangements or actions of the tools involved.

Ectoplasm: A substance formed by psychic mediums that can be used by people in the world of the spirit to take form.

Empath: A psychic who focuses on feeling the emotions of other people.

Energy: See "Chi."

ESP: Extra-sensory perception.

Ethereal travel: Meditative journeying through the world with your mind without moving your actual body.

Grounding: Mental or physical action that you can take to affect your energetic state to become more relaxed and focused.

Higher self: The part of yourself that has spiritual wisdom or that is divine.

Hypnosis: The practice of putting oneself or a willing other into a highly suggestible mental state.

Medium: A psychic whose focus is often on connecting with the dead and spirit guides, often through channeling.

Meditation: The act of quieting your mind to exist in a state of relaxed reciprocity.

Namaste: An Indian greeting which roughly means, "the divinity in me perceives and greets the divinity in you."

Numerology: A system of divination in which numbers are noticed or calculated and associated with specific meanings.

Ogham: A set of sticks with symbols etched or marked on them which are used as a system of divination.

Omen: A natural or accidentally occurring event that is taken to have symbolic meaning.

Pendulum: A plumb-bob, used in divination, whose movements when dangled from one's hand are used to amplify psychic answers.

Precognitive dreaming: Having a dream that predicts a future event that happens during your waking life.

Probability: A mathematical analysis of the likelihood that a random event or condition will happen.

Psychic: A person who is in tune with phenomena or information that is perceived from non-physical or even supernatural sources.

Runes: A set of stones etched or marked with symbols which are used as a system of divination.

Scrying: A form of divination in which the practitioner looks for visual images in a tool such as a crystal ball, a bowl of water or milk, a scrying mirror, or fire.

Séance: A group mediumship session, usually performed in the presence of the bereaved, often including channeling.

Square breathing: Breathing in for four counts, holding your breath for four more, breathing out for four counts, and then holding for four more before repeating.

Spirit guides: Entities with which a psychic medium can communicate. They are often thought to have once been living people who chose before we were born to help us through life.

Symbol: A word or picture of one thing that represents something else.

Tarot: A deck of seventy-eight cards used for divination.

Telepathy: Connecting one person's mind to another in order to share thoughts.

Bibliography

Campbell, Joseph. *Myths To Live By.* New York: Penguin Putnam, 1972.

———. *The Hero With a Thousand Faces.* New York: Bollingen Foundation, 1949.

Cunningham, Scott. *Divination for Beginners.* St. Paul, Minnesota: Llewellyn Publications, 2003.

Delsarte, François, and Genevieve Stebbins. *Delsarte System of Expression.* Charleston, SC: Nabu Press, 2010.

Eynden, Rose Vanden. *So You Want to Be a Medium.* Woodbury, MN: Llewellyn Publications, 2006.

Jung, Carl. *Man and His Symbols.* Garden City, NY: Doubleday & Company, 1964.

Luymes, Glenda. "Flagger in hospital after her truck struck by train in Langley." *The Vancouverite*. November 20, 2010. Accessed November 20, 2010 <http://www.vancouverite.com/2010/11/20/flag-person-fights-for-her-life-after-train-strikes-vehicle-in-langley/>

McElroy, Mark. *Lucid Dreaming for Beginners*. Woodbury, MN: Llewellyn Publications, 2007.

Powell, Diane. *The ESP Enigma: The Scientific Case for Psychic Phenomena*. New York: Walker Publishing Company, Inc., 2009.

Stockham, Rex A., Dennis L. Slavin, and William Kift. "The Specialized Use of Human Scent in Criminal Investigations." *Forensic Science Communications* volume 6, no. 3, July 2004. FBI. Accessed February 26, 2009 <http://www.fbi.gov/about-us/lab/forensic-science/communications/fsc/July2004/research/2004_03_research03.htm>

Thompson, Michelle. "Surviving Child Keeps Mom Going After Deadly Edmonton Crash." *Edmonton Sun*. Last Updated: May 10, 2010. Accessed November 20, 2010 <http://www.edmontonsun.com/news/edmonton/2010/05/04/13827146.html>

Crystal Ball Reading

For Beginners

Easy Divination & Interpretation

ALEXANDRA CHAURAN

Crystal Ball Reading for Beginners
Easy Divination & Interpretation
ALEXANDRA CHAURAN

Anyone can learn to use a crystal ball for divination, guidance, and meditation. This friendly introductory guide, written by a second-generation fortuneteller, is the only book available that focuses solely on the benefits of crystal ball reading. The author, a professional reader, presents everything you need to know to begin doing crystal ball readings immediately. You'll learn what a crystal ball is, how it works, and how to choose your first one. Step-by-step instructions describe what to look for when doing a reading and how to interpret the symbols found within the crystal ball. You can gain heightened intuitive abilities, greater self-knowledge, and a deeper understanding of the universe when you practice the ancient art of crystal ball reading.

978-0-7387-2626-7, 216 pp., 5³⁄₁₆ x 8   **$14.95**

So You Want to Be a MEDIUM?

A Down-to-Earth Guide

Rose Vanden Eynden

So You Want to Be a Medium?
A Down-to-Earth Guide
ROSE VANDEN EYNDEN

Are you fascinated by the spirit world? Wish you could communicate with loved ones on the Other Side? According to Spiritualist minister Rose Vanden Eynden, everyone possesses innate capabilities for spirit communication. Emphasizing the principles of modern Spiritualism, *So You Want to Be a Medium?* demonstrates how to enhance one's spiritual senses for working between worlds.

Through exercises involving meditation, breathing, dream work, symbols, and energy systems, the author teaches how to prepare one's mind and body for spiritual communication. Readers also learn about the many kinds of spirit guides and elemental energies, how to get in touch with them, and how to interpret their messages. Whether you're seeking to become a professional medium or simply interested in a closer connection to Creator, this fascinating guide to the spirit world can enrich your spiritual life—no matter what your religious background.

978-0-7387-0856-0, 288 pp., 6 x 9   **$16.95**

Aura Reading for Beginners
Develop Your Psychic Awareness for Health & Success
Richard Webster

When you lose your temper, don't be surprised if a dirty red haze suddenly appears around you. If you do something magnanimous, your aura will expand. Now you can learn to see the energy that emanates off yourself and other people through the proven methods taught by Richard Webster in his psychic training classes.

Learn to feel the aura, see the colors in it, and interpret what those colors mean. Explore the chakra system, and how to restore balance to chakras that are over- or under-stimulated. Then you can begin to imprint your desires into your aura to attract what you want in your life.

978-1-5671-8798-4, 208 pp., 5³⁄₁₆ x 8   **$12.95**

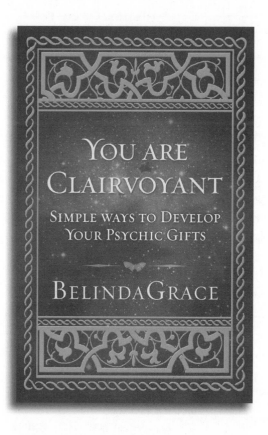

You Are Clairvoyant
Simple Ways to Develop Your Psychic Gifts
BELINDAGRACE

Clairvoyance is a gateway to unimagined possibilities—and it's within us all. Learn how to activate this powerful skill and use it to find greater happiness and fulfillment.

Anyone can connect with inner wisdom and divine guidance by following these simple techniques and easy exercises. On this enlightening path, you'll meet and talk to angels and spirit guides for assistance; gain insights into past lives to overcome negative patterns and find healing; conduct psychic conversations to get your point across; and get answers to important questions through automatic writing. This inspiring guide, written by a professional clairvoyant healer, features the author's true life stories and countless ways to use the gift of clairvoyance to transform your life—and yourself.

978-0-7387-2723-3, 240 pp., 5³⁄₁₆ x 8 **$14.95**

Astral Projection

For Beginners

Six Techniques for Traveling to Other Realms

EDAIN McCOY

Astral Projection for Beginners
Six Techniques for Traveling to Other Realms
EDAIN McCOY

Visit a realm in which time and space have no meaning—
the astral realm. This welcoming and friendly guide presents
step-by-step instructions for six easy and effective astral projection techniques.

Travel to different times and eras, visit with departed
loved ones, and explore different astral worlds, such as the
faerie realm. On the astral plane, it's also possible to heal
yourself, send healing energy to others, receive direction from
your spirit guides, and view your Akashic records, the astral
record of each soul's past and future events.

978-1-56718-625-3, 264 pp., 5³⁄₁₆ x 8   **$12.95**

Discover *your* Psychic Type

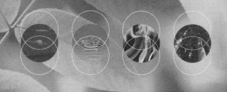

Developing and Using Your Natural Intuition

SHERRIE DILLARD

Discover Your Psychic Type
Developing and Using Your Natural Intuition
SHERRIE DILLARD

Intuition and spiritual growth are indelibly linked, according to professional psychic and therapist Sherrie Dillard. Offering a personalized approach to psychic development, this breakthrough guide introduces four different psychic types and explains how to develop the unique spiritual capabilities of each.

Are you a physical, mental, emotional, or spiritual intuitive? Take Dillard's insightful quiz to find out. Discover more about each type's intuitive nature, personality, potential physical weaknesses, and more. There are guided meditations for each kind of intuitive, as well as exercises to hone your psychic skills. Remarkable stories from the author's professional life illustrate the incredible power of intuition and its connection to the spirit world, inner wisdom, and your higher self.

978-0-7387-1278-9, 288 pp., 5³⁄₁₆ x 8   **$14.95**

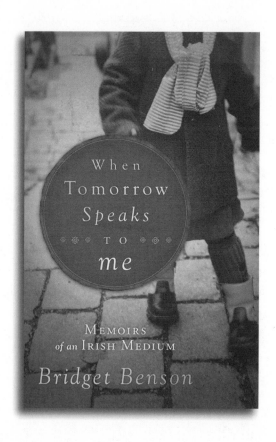

When
Tomorrow
Speaks
❖ TO ❖
me

MEMOIRS
of an IRISH MEDIUM

Bridget Benson

When Tomorrow Speaks to Me
Memoirs of an Irish Medium
Bridget Benson

Tragic deaths, secret love affairs, and powerful messages from the spirit world have colored Bridget Benson's life. She grew up in the small Irish farming village of Straide, County Mayo, a county of lush meadows and peat bogs, purple heather-clad moorland, and sandy-beached lakes. Bridget lived with her eight siblings, parents, grandparents, and great aunt in a house with no electricity or running water. When her grandma died on her seventh birthday, Bridget received a message that her beloved father, who also had "the gift," would die when she was twelve years old, and that she would carry on as the family seer.

When Tomorrow Speaks to Me tells the story of Bridget Benson's remarkably spiritual life, from her childhood experiences with spirit guides, ghosts, fairies, and leprechauns to the development of her career as a successful full-time medium.

978-0-7387-2106-4, 240 pp., 5³⁄₁₆ x 8   **$15.95**

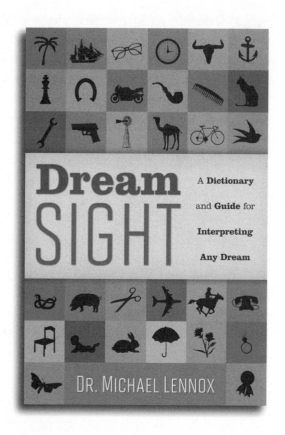

Dream SIGHT

A Dictionary and **Guide** for **Interpreting** Any Dream

DR. MICHAEL LENNOX